MEDITATIONS I

"You think you've read it all, as a track and/or cross country coach you most likely have, BUT not in this manner. Coach Neugebauer takes you back to those special memories of championships, just misses, dropped batons, DQ's and school and state records! A must read for the coach, athlete and parent to relive and understand what an athlete that runs/jumps/throws goes through every season. Sit back and let the memories come alive in the powerful and colorful prose of "Coach Dunn"!

–Andy Carr

XC & T&F Coach, Milton HS/Atlanta Track Club Events Team
LDR Record Keeper & Master Level Official, USA Track & Field

"Dunn Neugebauer is a highly motivated beneficiary of the running scene. He, personally, has made his own life joyous through his participation in and studying of running; but has also given much to his colleagues and student-athletes. He is a creative writer with motivation as a main goal of his publications."

–Jerry Crockett

Hall of Fame Track & Field/Cross Country Coach, Oklahoma State University

"Dunn's essays are very inspiring and remind me of my daily interactions of current and former athletes. He encompasses what it is like to be a coach to these truly amazing young adults."

–Jason Scott

Harrison High School cross country/track coach,
coach of MANY state championship teams

"I pray this will be read by many so they may have the benefit of Dunn's writing."

–Joe Tribble

Cross Country/Track Coach at Westminster,
also coach of MANY state championship teams

"Dunn's stories are like going for a run. Sometimes the route is straight and the destination clear. But most times, the path rolls up and down, and just when you think you know what is around the corner, you are surprised by what you find. Some stories are like point to point runs where you end up in a new destination. Others are round trips, where you end up at the place you started, but with a new perspective."

–Alan Drosky

Georgia Tech Head Cross Country/Track Coach

"*Meditations from the Finish Line* is the perfect read for coaches, athletes, parents and fans of the track and field community. It is a must have if you are passionate about the sports of cross country and track and field."

–Stephen Jayaraj

Cross Country/Track & Field Coach at Holy Innocents' in Atlanta
Founder of the Running Project

"When Dunn is coaching, he is always there for his athletes. He brings that same attention to his writing. Dunn's tales of running and life are always thought provoking and inspirational."

–Jackie Addy

Former high school state cross country champion; current cross country/track runner at the University of Florida

"What happens when a sportswriter becomes a participant in an athletic activity? And then a coach of it; what results? Brilliant observations flow across the paper. Dunn has done it here better than most."

–Coach Roy Benson

Author, former Marist School and UFla coach, founder of SMRC

MEDITATIONS FROM THE FINISH LINE

To Phil Wenzel!

30 years of friendship and counting!

6·24·21

FROM THE AUTHOR OF

FUNNY CONVERSATIONS WITH GOD
– AN UNCALLED-FOR DIALOGUE

ROCK BOTTOM, THEN UP AGAIN
– AND OTHER SPIRITUAL ESSAYS

WITS, WISDOMS, AND WONDERS…
FOR NAVIGATING THIS THING CALLED LIFE

MEDITATIONS FROM THE FINISH LINE

DUNN NEUGEBAUER

Mountain Arbor
Press

Alpharetta, GA

ISBN: 978-1-6653-0236-4 – Paperback
eISBN: 978-1-6653-0237-1 – eBook

Library of Congress Control Number:

Printed in the United States of America 0 6 1 0 2 1

♾This paper meets the requirements of ANSI/NISO Z39.48-1992 (Permanence of Paper)

Author photos by Bill Ponder

To my dad

For infusing me with this running gene thing – though I'm still pretty mad at you since you always got to stop after just one mile...

CONTENTS

THE WARM UP

I came up as a tennis player, though one day - tired of chasing down overheads, diving for passing shots, and arguing over line calls - I traded in my Stan Smith's for a pair of Nikes and was introduced to the adventures of the distance runner.

And adventures there were and still are, as what began as a quest to run my first marathon and qualify for Boston, led to coaching, competing, and afterwards racing to my notepad to write it all down. In fact, I can almost say it has led to everything. Trail magic perhaps could be an understatement, as to this day I run through the Georgia trails by a river, get passed by the deer, stared at by squirrels, and sometimes get lapped even by the slowest of turtles.

Still, the sound of my footsteps and the whisper of the river keep moving me forward – hopefully always will.

You could say that distance running became an entry point to my very soul, regardless of my physical shape, and this is particularly so now as I get older when the mile markers are disappearing behind my feet at a much slower pace.

I'm a coach at a high school currently – working with cross country and track kids. Still, I will never refer to myself as a "coach," but instead a bumper on the bumper pool table, or perhaps the Coral Reefer Band to our school's Jimmy Buffett.

And I'm good with that, because I think a lot of growing up is a case study in self-awareness – learning what you can and can't do and conversely spending as much time as possible doing things you enjoy, things you're good at.

In moving on, the written word has always attracted me – to me a game isn't complete until I've sat down and chopped the two-hour event down to 16 sentences or so. In that vein, I'm happy to say that running has led me to a lot more than that – the introspection of it all, the gains and pains of staring at that precious watch after crossing a finish line, the pain of a hard train, the bonding at the coffee shops soon thereafter.

During the pandemic – when the world was shut down and there was a padlock around my very school and office, we – and myself – were forced to look inside and see what really makes us tick. What do we love? And who? And why? What gets you out of bed when you can no longer do what used to be normal? Who are you?

And during this, I found that most of my stories – at least the ones that made me push other chores off to the side and get to the typewriter – were about running. One day, my co-Coach – the above mentioned 'Jimmy Buffett' – said this to me: "Put these in a book."

Maybe I just like the simplicity of the thought, nothing hidden – like the naked feeling on the last mile when your intentions are good, but the gas tank is empty. Still, you plod on, exposed to the universe, pleading to the God you believe in while willing to sacrifice the allotted three goats to get you across that sacred finish line.

In looking at it all - and there's no getting around this – when the run is over, I always feel better, because even the horrible workouts are great because the mental trash has been taken out, left back around mile #3 or #4 or wherever.

Enough from me. After all, if you're a true runner, you don't want to hear a lot of intro – there's nothing worse than long-winded race starters. As I explained to one lost soul who told an April Fool's joke at the starting line of an April 1st race, "the only thing runners want to hear is a firing gun."

I was one of those runners and I get it. Hopefully, you do, too.

Enough said. The gun is fired. Enjoy the run…

–Dunn Neugebauer
Holder of lots of jobs
Author, coach, nice guy

PART I: THE STARTING LINE

0:00:00

A RUNNER'S PRAYER

Dear Lord, please don't let me get spiked in the ankle again. That REALLY hurt when that kid clipped me in Darlington.

And please don't let me throw up nor be thrown up upon. My mother is not a runner, dear Lord, so when I presented my singlet for her to wash, she really didn't understand how I got second hand Doritos and chili from a simple Saturday 3.1-mile run.

And please don't let me get thrown around after the gun goes off. I only weigh 84 pounds, sometimes those big kids don't respect that, particularly when they're chasing bling, adulation, and hearing their names called out at Monday's assemblies.

Please deliver me from cramps, whether for 'girl reasons' or from race pains, and please get me in and out of the bathrooms beforehand where I can quickly breathe your wonderful freely given air.

And deliver me not next to inexperienced runners. After all, these are the ones that eat the Doritos and the chili.

Please help me beat my rival, particularly when she taunted me at the last race with a T-shirt that read, "Don't bother with the course map, just follow me!" I'm all for confidence and creativity Dear Lord, but I think that's taking it a bit too far.

Please give me my own seat on the bus. Despite it being a small, 14-passenger thing, somehow it seems to seal in every piece of sweat on every single singlet. (Please see above "throw up" part for emphasis.)

Going backwards, please wake me up on time, and

soothe my mind before I throw the alarm clock across the room when I see it's only 5:15 on a Saturday. And please forgive me both now, and forever more, the cuss words I scream when asking myself why I got into this silly sport in the first place, and why I can't be normal and play the games that start at 4 p.m.

Speaking of, and in going forward, could you consider making me normal? Running until you're dizzy and almost passing out – something doesn't quite sound right about all that.

Please deliver us short-winded race starters, guns that don't fire blanks, kids that don't fall where we have to do it all over again, and I promise I'll be okay as long as there is something to drink at the finish line.

Please deliver me my pillow for the morning trip, as falling asleep tilted funny against those windows leaves me with a crick in my neck that lasts until Tuesday.

Please let this be the Saturday that John and Billy have to carry the tent – I had to do it the last two times – or at least please fix the wheels on that cart-thing where I can just put it on that.

And please deliver me a bagel – just a bagel. Pre-race eggs don't seem to stay down very well, coffee hurts when I spill it on my lap, so a bagel is easy to carry and it's never – as of yet – come back up, even when my coach is telling me to sprint the last 150 meters.

Speaking of, please don't let my coach run beside me during the race and yell at me in the last 150 meters. It makes me cry and he gets REALLY mad when I yell back.

Please don't let me forget my shoes and leave them on that tarp again. Last time I did that, mom yelled. It also made me cry.

And deliver me not unto hornet's nests, bee stings, elbows to my rib cage, and twisted ankles. These are things that make me scream, the crying completely optional.

Please pick me back up when I collapse in the finish chute. And extra prayers for those who work in those things – the ones who pick us up with our sweat and our blood and our puke. And my second-hand Doritos and chili on my singlet.

And finally, please forgive my teacher who almost didn't let me out of class last Wednesday. He said this wasn't even a sport, even sneered when he said it. I give thanks on this day, Oh Lord, for keeping me from punching him right square in the face.

It is in these things and plenty more that I will keep asking, day after day, mile after mile, race after race. In Your name I pray…

A-men.

TWICE A RUNNER

I choose to tell my own story, not because I'm a braggart, but more that I'm too lazy to do research. Some love to sit in libraries surrounded by papers, magazines, periodicals – smoke wisping off their still-hot coffee while they settle in for a Sunday.

To quote from a Jack Nicholson movie, "I'd rather stick needles in my eyes."

Instead, this tale brings me back to an old two-lane – and describing it that way does the road a favor – as it was an old 'sort of asphalt but not quite dirt' lane that branched off of 441 between Madison, Georgia and Rutledge, wended its way to a dead end before, in front of you, stood what used to be a school.

It's sad, really, seeing those walls gone – those walls that used to hold so many emotions. Stress from tests not studied for, lusts from older girls you'd never make out with, nervousness having to sit through last class before suiting up for the big game, anger at him or her for whatever reason.

Sadder still, I'm standing on what used to be a track – a dirt track – with the former starting line drawn in the mud with a coach's foot, leaving the runner not really sure if he or she were finished or not. Someone would stop you, or so you hoped, and you'd check your watch to let yourself know whether you were happy, sad, or somewhere in between.

My dad used to watch me run – and I'd like to think I made him proud that day when I crossed an invisible finish line on what was then simply called the 2-mile run. You see, in football season I didn't carry the ball for 124 yards on 17 carries, nor did I throw it for more than that.

Instead, I'd spent afternoons distinguishing a red headed woodpecker from a red bellied one, charting in my journal that I'd seen two rufous sided towhees, and would clean the glass off my binoculars instead of getting the blood and guts out of my cleats.

The macho had their football practices. I had Alfred Hitchcock and the Three Investigator books, with the Hardy Boys fast on deck. And, of course, my birds.

Funny what you remember: In the 12-mile drive to school, I'd look out the window and count the birds. One day I saw 34 – 21 of them red winged blackbirds that sat on wires or darted over a Madison pond. The record was 78, I think, but only me knew or cared

In fact, it's been almost 50 years, and this is the first time I've mentioned it. To anyone. Besides, this may be "colorful" now to have known what an ornithologist actually was. Back in 1975, however, it would've perhaps drawn a beating – definitely a mocking that would've led to my red face and less chance at a good date for Homecoming.

Back to the track: It's overgrown now, with grass I can almost describe as weeds. There's no trace of dirt; the ground not even level anymore, though the lack of evidence of the former sweat of speed workouts and long runs don't give way as easily – even with 45 years of Mother Nature doing her work.

Goosebumps rise on my arms while I stand here. Tears of frustration, qualifying for state, not beating my rival, it's all here, right here, and I have to remain even longer at my genesis of becoming a runner.

That term: runner. You either get it or you don't. A

funny memory of how I knew I was hooked: One day someone recited my mile time and he was a second off. I quickly corrected him. He, not a runner, looked at me with this, "what difference does it make," expression.

Oh, the silly fool. Each second is earned out here, time is won and lost, but when you win, you want your credit, damn it, and if you have to fight and kick and spit for the second, you do it.

There, I feel better already.

And later in my life, when I REALLY knew I was hooked – the day my wife told me she wanted a divorce. My first thought? "Oh well, I guess I'll go run four mile repeats at tempo pace, then a cool down."

I laugh at that memory, though I can assure you she herself did not. Still, my brain remains on overload, not just at starting guns and all that happened thereafter, but it's also those walls – those walls that aren't there.

It was there I learned that the only sure things in life were that when two drunks start wrestling, they always end up fighting. And you can never throw up only once. And the two most boring things in the country were a Latin class lecture and the drone of a golf announcer's voice.

But it is here – right where I stand - where my dad's genes spliced into my very own, and right over there – right there by that big rock – is where he warned me of the perils of going out too fast on the first lap.

And maybe I should've known even then that I was a runner. After all, I went out too fast anyway.

Guess what else? You probably did, too…

A MAN AT A FINISH LINE

It's funny how the memory works...

Eight years – it's been eight years since I saw that old man at the finish line at Westminster. White hair. Probably 85 years old. Spry, very agile despite the years. That quick smile for everyone who approached. The staccato laugh.

Eight years and I still can see him, have a perfect JPEG in my head of all who approached, hugged, high-fived him, wished him well, patted him on the back. Eight years – and this memory of mine – the one that can't recall if I've washed my hair when I'm in the shower; or if I've taken my Juice Plus or not, even though I'm standing – RIGHT THERE – in front of both of the bottles.

I even had to develop a system: Bring the first bottle forward. Take the pill. Push it back. Bring the other bottle forward. Take it. Push it back.

Anyway, it was a cross country meet Wednesday after school. Their coaches were always good enough to invite us – perhaps some combination of us being nice people, in close proximity to their school, and maybe simply because they had the athletes that could kick a hundred percent of our butts.

Whatever the reason, we were there – always were – and this tale begins with my standing at the finish line, yellow pad in hand, going through the times I'd just recorded. Our kids had just finished – spit, blood, and drool coming out of their adolescent faces – some sprinting it home, some who started like a Porsche and ended up a Pinto, others who simply took it as a joy run.

Cross country at my school was and is a no-cut sport,

you see, so we attract all types – and I can't put the word "all" in big and dark enough font to make my point. We had a 15:58 top runner and a 36.42 last one – we had several with college dreams, we had others who walked even during the warmup while they flirted and griped about chemistry class and why were they having so many quizzes.

Regardless, I clock them all – record it in my notebook for all eternity – or at least until I run out of pages and stuff the pad on my shelf at home with all the others. There are years on that shelf, faces long forgotten, times the runners themselves no longer remember, pages I won't even look through.

Still, writing – for me – must happen. It's a way of knowing that the race occurred; perhaps a method of making sense of all this. Fortunately, my shelf is running out of room for notebooks, each one pushing the other further down, as if its newness to the pile makes it the most important, the king of the hill if you will.

But the man. At the finish line. Just on the other side of the finish chute from me.

He had on shorts – his bony knees stuck out as far as his shoes did. He wore a T-shirt promoting some race that happened two or three presidents ago. There was a cap on his head – Slippery Rock it was, and being a southern boy, I'd heard of the school but couldn't tell you where it was with a gun to my head.

I couldn't help noticing, though, that the kids all made it a point to go talk to him, give him a high-five, a quick hug. He was an attractor factor, and even the racers who'd barely glanced and digested the numbers on their watch made him as important as the digits that – for better or for worse – always dictate the mood of the true runner.

He was glad to see each and every one of them – this boy, that girl, those parents. You can always tell, you know? A lot of people you're talking to are looking someplace else, or checking their watch, or fidgeting a bit. Planning their escape…

He wasn't like that; not even close. He was in, all in, at each encounter. Unlike most people, where everywhere you are NOT is the place to be, he was the opposite of that. He was very… present… that's perhaps the best word I could use.

So there I stand, I'm separated from him by two lines of police tape that had designated the path the runners had just taken. It was a simple step over, or under – he was maybe 12, 15 feet away. A man of routine I am - usually at this point I head back to our tent, remind the kids to do a cool down, tell them again to clean up all the crap they've managed to build up even though we'd been here less than three hours.

At a cross country race, the tent resembles a living room after a robbery. There is crap. Everywhere! Bags on top of shoes on top of books on top of wallets – yes, wallets! – on top of warmups. There are shirts, and spike kits and med kits, and pillows. Some kids bring half their bedroom to a race – though in their defense we do get up AWFUL early – and on a Saturday most of the time.

Gatorade bottles, water, all the containers tilted – most of it spilt out – leaving that poor tarp that we bought on the fly at Sam's one morning already getting tested despite the early season. Power Bars – or what's left of them – and "race food" – some of it eaten, some not – are all scattered among the above debris.

But I keep getting away from this man. Actually, I had to move towards him – as big of a creature of habit as I am. Now, really quick: I'm not an intrusive man – I see no reason to barge into your life with my handshake and/or my resume. There's generally no reason you should know me, as I choose to live gently, in flow, like the Chattahoochee River I run past most mornings.

On this day, at that finish line, however, I couldn't NOT do this. There was no shyness in my steps; suddenly I was a man of purpose. A motto always rears up in my head when I approach anyone – whether for a polite chit chat or going back in the college days when trying to hit on a woman: Approach with confidence or don't approach at all. Period. Go big or go home.

He saw me as I lifted the second piece of tape. Still, there was no alarm in his demeanor – in Atlanta you never know what people want – but he stood in peace, perhaps a bit curious.

When I faced him head on, it was his eyes that drew me in. They were eyes that had seen much, yet a twinkle remained in his. Yes, he had seen thousands and thousands of days, but his peaceful gaze told him he was glad to be around on THIS day. Now. Here.

I patted him on the shoulder while his gaze drew me in like magnets; perhaps a timeline was going through his skull about when or if we'd met. People say you can't see the wheels spinning in people's heads. I contend that you can. We hadn't met, though, for the record. I'd have known it, though I do get the irony, this is coming from the memory of the shower/wash-the- hair and the taking-the-vitamins thing.

"I'm going to be you one day, sir. You inspire me."

He appeared taken back – just for a micro-second. Just when you think you've heard it all, you realize that you haven't. Still, his wisdom won out and he smiled. He knew I meant it. He knew I was harmless. He took it as the compliment that it was and remains to this very day.

"Thank you, sonny," he said. The eye-twinkle got larger, he patted me on my shoulder. Then, just like that, I was gone.

As these years have passed, I'm glad to this very day that I did NOT have a conversation with him, didn't find out his name. A funny statement, perhaps, but knowing his name and occupation would've diminished it somehow; would've had me compartmentalizing and categorizing him with others I knew in his job, or someone I'd met where he lived.

I'm glad I didn't do that – even now. And I never saw him again, for the record, even though I've been back on that campus several times. Funnier still, I find no reason to look for him – our brief intersection served its purpose.

He was a man at a finish line, whose eyes had seen many days, but he was glad to see THIS day. He was a man who people just wanted to say hi to, just give him a smile. He was a man with knobby knees and a Slippery Rock baseball hat and an old T-shirt.

But it was a face and I smile I won't and haven't forgotten…and that is and always will be quite enough…

CROSS COUNTRY UTOPIA

It's all here in front of you: runners and coaches lugging tents, tarps, coolers and wagons. Kids gathering around waiting for their medals. Race directors poring over results, making sure they can pronounce all the names right; checking to make sure they hang the right bling on the right neck at the right time.

Earlier in the morning you had to laugh. After all, this is the only sport in the world that can cause a major traffic tie-up at 5:30 on a Saturday morning, literally, in the middle of nowhere. You're driving through East Bumble, fearing you've gotten your team lost, and then – viola – up ahead are bus brake lights, car windows being rolled down to get directions from some guy or gal holding a cup of coffee, soon to be pointing fingers, directing, guiding.

And an earlier morning conversation: One of your runners approached and said, "Coach, we have to be the weirdest kids in the school. We get up at 5 on Saturday morning!"

Yes, we do. But think about it, every sport has its nuance. You play basketball? Then prepare to give up your Thanksgiving and Christmas holidays. Baseball? So much for Spring Break. Football? Your summer is in the weight room, culminated by three days in Camp Hell, lived out in fields complete with dust and bugs and heat.

On this day, the race director is smart enough not to have the awards near the porta-johns. You stand behind him on purpose, getting this view – these kids in anticipation, these parents using their cell phones as cameras, grandparents with smiles so big their teeth touch both ears.

Fortunately, some of your kids' names are called – they left their kidneys and spleens back at Mile 2 but – in the beauty of the cross country kid – they kept going anyway. This sport attracts the best in your humble opinion. Why? Because we all sweat, suffer, sometimes trip, always get up.

And whether you were first or last or somewhere in between, the applause and the appreciation and the cameras were flashing just the same. You may not stand on the podium, but you did it. You achieved.

The last neck has accepted the last medal now. The above tents and tarps and wagons are being pulled up a hill, past a parking lot. You are praying your bus driver is still there. Life will continue with a cat nap, college football to watch, dinner plans for later.

It's cross country Saturday morning, that's what it is. The only way to understand it is to do it – to hear the alarm every Saturday and wonder just what in the hell you were thinking? But, like the above runners, you get up, turn off your alarm, off you go.

Former basketball star Scott Skiles once said that basketball fans are like churchgoers – many attend, but few understand. Yeah, ditto that with cross country.

On the bus home, coaches are already on Milesplit – they have been since seconds after the race. Kids are asleep. The bus gears shift, protest, but like the runners, grind forward. You used to wonder what you were getting into; did you really want to give up your Saturdays?

You laugh. Because you do get it. And better still, you know. This is exactly what Saturday mornings were made for…

COMPREHENSIVELY CARROLLTON

You stand at the season's final exam in Carrollton and it is very comprehensive. The road wasn't easy - coronavirus cancellations, Georgia mixed weather, and the typical drama of any season all jockeyed for position to get inside your team's heads.

Still, here you are, after your team has aced its way through PRs at the Asics Invitationals and the Coach Woods of the world – and you watched and listened as the kids bragged about their finishes, wore their medals like muscles before assemblies, wrote their times in ink as another goal to top.

As for now, though, you stand below Separation Slope, and both of those S's are capitalized for a reason. It's 17 steps for the record - only 17 - but during that trek that must be made twice is where dreams are made and dreams go to fade.

You remember one runner - about to win a state title - who never recovered, and when he collapsed before starting up the final hill you don't recall ever willing somebody forward more strenuously. You called on Jesus and even greats from other religions, offered silently to sacrifice some of your very own blood - but none got that wonderful soul back up again.

Carrollton - where you don't leave the same person you were when you arrived - at least you don't if you have the guts to do it right. You toss and turn not only the night before but the week before because you remember it was right THERE where that girl passed you or it was THAT spot where you overtook that kid. Go easy on yourself if you didn't excel, by the way. It means you qualified, to begin with, you persevered, and the fact that you can't sleep means you simply give a damn.

In moving on, it was over there where a co-coach and friend danced in front of the scorer's table – he'd pulled the results off the computer before they were even declared unofficial. He'd survived an illness and his first test back in life was the adrenaline of Carrollton and that slope thing again and all those hills.

It was over here you celebrated with your girls once - they got in a puppy huddle and face timed an alum, a master's grad of the Carrollton Course, and your school. She had already conquered state individually, knew the feeling of breaking that sacred tape, but her team had never known that, so when she answered her phone and saw her state champ teammates breaking the news, she put her hands over her face and she cried.

You were in that huddle; you did, too. You see, you don't leave Carrollton unscathed, nor should you. If you do, you didn't do it right, and when you get in your car and drive away, the bigger the knot in your stomach the better you did, regardless of the results.

There's another spot that hits home - right there behind the start and below the porta-a-johns. One of your runners heard the good news and lost it on the spot. You congratulated her with a quick hug - she with happy tears and you realize you had a hand in it.

It was the Picture That Was Never Taken, in your eyes, and that's too bad because pictures don't just say 1,000 words, they also climb into your very soul sometimes, follow you when you shop and go to movies and try to sleep.

You remember approaching seven boys at the starting line once, trying to inject your adrenaline from the past

14 years. "Is there any place else you'd rather be?" you scream. You'll never forget one kid - that sophomore - who thought about that for a moment before answering, "Well, I hear New Zealand is nice this time of year."

Okay, it wasn't what you were looking for, but why shouldn't funny things happen in Carrollton, too? Adrenaline, after all, comes out in oh so many ways, and at the strangest of times.

So, now you're back on the bus and this time there are no state banners to raise, the top rung of the podium again denied. Still, though your body is in the second row, your spirit is still out there, yelling at those beautiful souls to climb those 17 steps, not to get caught up in the too-fast start, stay strong for the second loop.

The season is over now, but it's not. It's really not.

Because there are memories of laughing and crying and dancing and face timing loved ones. There are podium steps climbed and podium steps denied. There are ankles twisted, runners collapsing, happy and sad tears.

And there's a JPEG in your skull - of a photo that was never taken - therefore leaving Carrollton is never a wait till next year - not really - because with everything that happens, there is so much forever imprinted into your skull.

And it is exactly those pictures that serve as connect-the-dot memories that drive you back - one day, and one training run at a time.

See you next year...

VALEDICTORY ADDRESS TO THE RUNNING CLASS OF 2020

This may not be what you want to hear, but what I want to say to you is one word: Congratulations!

Now you graduate... virtually and/or eventually, surviving hopefully a one-time-only race. It wasn't what you trained for, it didn't require hill work, mile repeats, or quarters at tempo pace. And no, you didn't get to qualify for state. Still, you learned so much more. You didn't sacrifice for your teammates or for your pride, you sacrificed to save people's lives. Your PRs were put on hold, they don't matter for now.

What you've done is way more than any number that appears on a watch once the finish line is crossed. You've just performed for a larger audience than 20 or 30 teammates and three or four coaches. And unlike most races, where only one breaks the tape, this time you all did.

You will all go down as hopefully the only class EVER to go through this. There aren't medals shiny enough to enshroud your deserving necks. Though now, you hear phrases like "time you can't get back," and "it ended so abruptly," one day this will be replaced with "You're from the Class of 2020! Tell me about that!"

Maybe it was like the mile. The first lap you had no clue what you were getting into, if you could even do this. The second lap you had to develop a new stride, find a rhythm never before found, invent a gear not currently in your training plan. The third lap, a new you was born.

Maybe you can do this, maybe we all can. Maybe

we're almost there. On the fourth and final lap, you saw an end in sight, a finish line of sorts. This one moved, though; bobbed and weaved with the changing of every newsbreak, but it was out there. Like the runner that you are, you simply moved towards it.

You see, you can alter the rules, vary the course, constantly mess with the finish line, but you can't change the runner. What's in your soul is there, and it will always move ahead. Even now, with the end unsure, you just keep going. Lap four, hopefully, is ending soon. But congrats to all of you because you'll keep moving anyway. There will be plenty more races to train for -- some of them local, many out of town, this one world-wide.

And guess what? One day soon you'll cross a finish line that's never been crossed, in a race never before held. You will be remembered, as you dang well should. Most people train for events with course maps, guidelines, rules, restrictions, and an order of finish. You had none of that. So, great job to you all. Your time will never, can never, be broken, official computerized scoring or no.

You all just made history. And there isn't a podium alive that's big enough to hold you.

Congratulations. Seriously… congratulations!

I WEAR THE RING

I wear the ring; I wear the ring and it signifies a rung on the ladder of trying to be a better coach, a better person, while at the same time being around a group of kids who – when you get right down to it – continue to save me.

Even though trophies in days past have resulted in ego and in me, it is this one – the most coveted one – that does not. It sits in a drawer where it has been for 19 months – I pull it out on days when I need a reminder, when the steps through the hallways require more pep, passion, more life.

Regardless, it brings back a day when I stood at the bottom of a hill in some place called Carrollton, Georgia and I saw all that, felt that and more, and fulfilled my job requirements by writing a number next to seven names, on a pad I got from our supply cabinet at work.

There's a picture of those seven, as they posed after the fact with medals and shirts and smiles, braces on some of the young teeth, hair tied, cheeks painted with our school insignia. I use that picture as my screensaver often, not necessarily because of athletic life but for life in general.

There's this one – the freshman – who ironically hates running, hates it. And after this title she never took a jogging step until the first day of practice the following fall. Still, she's spry and athletic and for some reason, she's good at it.

On that day, this verb – I'll always think of her that way – flew down that last hill and passed a couple of soon-to-be Division I runners. You'd think that'd be enough, right? It wasn't. I watched while she waited in the finish chute, where she'd pick the fallen up, wrap her skinny arm around another and walked her through.

It is that quality right THERE that puts a lump in my throat – even now after the seasons have changed again and again. Some emotions come straight back up – forever non-tainted – and if there were an alcoholic beverage in me at the end of a day, I could always feel a tear about to drop.

So be it.

Right behind her was one who defeated her biggest opponent – her own Type-A self - as in the past, a clock that told her she didn't run a personal record resulted in tears of her own – even if the course was hilly, the temperature perhaps somewhere between bake and broil.

Something, somewhere along the way, snapped – or should I say unsnapped – and her smile signifies a personal win I hope she won't forget, particularly in this comparing society that demands you be perfect, the best, always at 100-percent.

Rubbish I say – always 100-percent doesn't exist – on some days you're lucky to get 90 or 80 or even 74 or lower. You just put out there what you have and let the chips fall where they may.

There's the next one with her knobby legs and her wired teeth, those legs that would be kicking soccer balls at goalies within two months. She shares a sport and good for her – and who invented this society where you're supposed to choose out of the womb anyway?

We sent her to soccer with not only a medal and a title, but a season that will stick with her even in future days of weddings and motherhood.

It's ironic that our #4 is sticking her head into the picture, because that's what she did in real life. She never ran her first three years of high school – except to stay fit for lacrosse. We'd pass at the river and we'd smile at each other. Still, it was her last year of high school when she remembered the joys of running in the middle grades, so back she came.

She was a self-coachable soul, forever reminding me that staying out of the way is often more important than stepping in, so when I suggested she work on her hills in mid-season, she simply smiled and said, "Don't worry, I live in a bumpy neighborhood."

Enough said. She did the work while I remained smart enough to leave her alone.

Our #5 is a converted swimmer – you can do that with running, you know? With football, baseball, or basketball, you usually know at an early age. With running, I'd bet the farm many grab high school diplomas without ever knowing they're good at it. This one, our deciding #5, gave it a try as a sophomore and realized her legs – used to outkick opponents in the pool – also were rather effective on hills.

And I'll speak of my #6 and #7 together, because they always are. These are two who shared the same lane on the track, in a sighting I can only describe as adorable. The same with bus seats, classroom arrangements, weekend plans.

They look like sisters though they are not – they are picture pretty, both inside and out, and it surprised me not at all to see one with the other while attacking the hills on the second loop. These two being seniors, it was these two I sought out immediately after learning the final result.

They were crying – it would perhaps be fitting if their tears were in sync – left eye, right eye, then both – and I couldn't help getting a lump in there myself. Besides, we'd cried the year before for a different reason – we were "proven" to be the best in the state and on that day, we were not that at all.

And one must never forget the alternates, the teammates, the ones not in "The 7" but the ones who still got up – day after day – and were there that day freezing and clapping and cheering. I was once asked my definition of JV sports and I'll share my answer here: "JV sports are exactly like boxing out in basketball. You do all the work, yet you don't get the final result. Still, it if weren't for you, it wouldn't have happened. In short, if you take them out of the equation, then you don't have the equation!"

There. That's the love I have for those people, those girls, those spectators, those moms and dads.

Moving on, this ring signifies a friend and coach, one who overcame a mental sickness during the season, one who had to leave us early, one who didn't expect to be back. There are pictures that will never leave my head, and if I live to be 242, I'll always see him dancing at the finish line, not giving a red damn what anyone said or thought, while he celebrated the fruits of his passions.

Sports are one thing, though it took my own battle with depression to realize the best victories don't result in trophies or medals or stories on the front page of the sports. No one calls your name out at assemblies; you celebrate the win the way you accomplished it – quietly. Often alone.

Some races are won inside, always internal, and when I see that man right there, dancing at that table, I know what a real victory is like, regardless of how good these seven wonderful creatures did.

Last but not least, I look to these people identified as assistant coaches. They are bumpers on bumper pool tables, the Coral Reefer Band to Jimmy Buffet. Still, take them away and what do you have? A regular season, followed by a passionless banquet, with a lot of eating, very little clapping, and an audience staring at their watches ready to get the hell out of there.

Behind every good coach exist even better assistants. There must be – life and sport simply demand it – require it even.

In signing off, I don't exactly know how to apologize for this. Maybe it's a combination of arrogance, self-bravado, mixed with a genuine love for seven tiny girls that ran faster than other team's seven tiny girls one day a couple Novembers past.

Maybe I'll never be able to explain it, why it makes me put these words to paper so many months later, after many teams have finished many seasons and signed off with their own post-season aftermaths.

Then again, maybe I don't have to explain it at all.

After all, I wear the ring…

THE POWER OF THE MOMENTS

The Buddhists always tell you to stay in the moment, but if you've been around cross country and track long enough, I'm not really sure that's possible.

It's sunny out now and as I wandered out to watch a couple of seniors do their workout, my mind exploded -- exhausted itself after the events of the things that have happened after so many starting guns have gone off over the years.

We lost the state 4 X 400 two years in a row by the combined length of a pencil eraser. My sophomore broke 20 minutes for the first time in her life in cross country. One of our seniors broke five in the mile at the Time Trial. Two years ago one of our runners described to me how the four high school years are EXACTLY like the four laps of a mile. Another kid, a former nine-minute miler, ran a 6:07 three years later.

You don't read much about 6:07 milers these days -- just know that if you're reading this, the kid earned it, deserved it, and his smile when looking at his watch made me melt in a good way.

Are guys supposed to hug each other? Sure they are ... just monitor the progress of a 9-minute miler turned 6:07.

I write this not as one to argue with the Buddhists -- or any spiritual or religious belief -- yet one who differs in a positive way. Let your mind go where it wants, as long as it's positive. When the moon's tilted right, I can still see that sophomore look at her watch, a 19:54 staring back at her. Can literally see not just her, but her mind celebrating in such joy, such accomplishment, such happiness.

I remember walking up to her just to be around it -- the fact that I got to help make it a positive experience times 12. It's not only why we do it, but the life lessons learned from watching them get it, whether the number on their watches makes them happy or not.

The moment, if I have to comply, centers around the firing of that gun -- a sound so absent last year after March 12 that I found myself turning on old western movies just to hear it again. Addicted, perhaps?

In moving on, I interviewed a coach of a different sport the other day, and he said something interesting, yet true.

"We don't let our kids get into a negative mindset if they're quarantined or get sent home. We remind them to be grateful to get another chance to play. After all, you never know if it could get taken away again."

Yeah. That. Exactly that.

And with that, I close in gratitude. And with a track meet looming ahead on our Saturday schedule. And with kids out on a Saturday putting in some miles, getting some extra stretching in.

It's these little snapshot moments, you know -- the ones that fill your head, make you smile, keep you going. And there is so much in those moments, so much adrenaline, hope, and positivity.

So whether present or not, whether the mind is traveling or it's where my feet are, please don't take the power of those moments away.

TO WATCHING KIDS FIND THEIR WINGS…

Finding your wings is no easy thing. Just when they begin to sprout, they are turned this way and that, bent, folded, by right and by wrong. Often, the young are left back on the landing strip – where they started – with less fuel and more confusion.

You have to have the bricks before you can build the house. Peer, educational, and social media often puts this backwards, making the young compare and contrast and hurry into something, only making our youth throw up their hands and wonder where? Why? What for?

I watch wings sprout every day, it's what I live for. Some open slower than others, creaking doors if you will – they are the ones who take a lot of practice runs before opening up to you, to me, to the world. Others take off quickly, bump their butts, get up quickly.

Still, in either a wink of an eye or an eternity, all are soon singing on the bus when you're taking them to the river. They sing loud and they sing badly – but I find myself turning down the radio and listening though I'm not really sure why.

You see, when angels sing it doesn't have to be on key. It's their uniqueness coming out, their little voices, and they mean no harm, they're just starting up their engines, on the launching pad if you will. As I've said, sometimes the biggest part of teaching and coaching is knowing when to shut the heck up and get out of the way. Period.

Besides, the literal definition of the word educate is to "draw out from, NOT to put into." I remind myself of that definition every day. Oh, how I wish others would do the same.

Moving on, there's one I had to give directions on how to run around a track. Not taking credit, but he's now running 18-minute 5Ks and captaining the team. Another drew tardy slips almost daily – once glued her own hands together – but in her spare time she'd drift off into a corner and write songs. One likes to swim, and once drew me a picture while in class.

The artistry was awful – the picture hangs on my office wall to this very day.

Flight paths are all around me as I walk from one class to another. Some start slower than others. Many, by age alone, are cleared for takeoff whether they want to go or not.

I recall my own 20s, going through the trial and error of teaching tennis, selling pots and pans, banking, multi-level marketing – often hitting the bed at night with no energy and less money. Then one night I asked one question: Why exactly is it that you can type 90 words a minute?

Not bragging, because I had nothing to do with it. Literally nothing.

And there was that day as a freshman at Berry College, sitting in a classroom learning how to write a resume. The Objective part had me stumped, and I put my pencil down while the whole class scribbled furiously. "How do you (bleeping) know!" I wanted to scream.

It's the cosmic joke. You search everywhere only to find it within the whole time. You could shorten the time, but God wants you to enjoy his humor while you find your rhythm, experience, waddle, crash and burn.

In closing, I'll crank up the bus again today – there will be 14 or so on board. They may sing – will probably destroy every song from Johnny Cash to Led Zeppelin. I recall one day being disappointed when one of my youth brought his music with him. In all due respect to the Beatles and the Cars, I wanted to hear him – and them!

Still, on some nights, when the moon is tilted funny, I'll think of tardy slips, once shy kids, the struggle of bricks and houses and resumes. Will remember shutting out all the exterior voices and simply asking a question to the person in the mirror. Will see smoke from crashes with no black boxes in sight, the smiles of an A on a test, the pains of being rejected.

Just as often, I'll turn the radio down and I'll hear singing. It'll be bad, off-key, yet so simply angelic.

And I will laugh. At least, that is, until I perhaps start to cry…

AN ODE TO RUNNING

My dad was a distance runner at New Hampshire and, except for the speed, strength, and kick part, he passed some of those genes down to me. I'll never forget our "Field of Dreams, Kevin Costner playing-catch-with-dad moment" when he pulled me aside before the two-mile run.

"Don't go out too fast, it's eight laps. Stay relaxed, it's not how you start, it's how you finish."

The gun went off, and I – sporting new, blue shoes, some new zits, and a body weighing about a buck-10, went out way too fast. Still, the stubbornness that is me is another story for another time. Or better yet maybe not.

This isn't to bore you with my marathon stories – running three days after a colonoscopy, getting gummy bears stuck in a bad place after one dropped into my shorts, finally qualifying for Boston despite hugging the Wellesley girls way too long at Mile 13, or hanging it up in Twin Cities after barfing up a lung on Mile 22.

Today I ran with someone I coached six years ago. I always know when they truly get running when they do NOT spout off times, distances, paces and races. It's the bonding, the brotherhood, the people. How he just saw Andy the other day; ran with Will; caught up with Warner, and how is so-and-so doing?

There is a period in a runner's life when the final number is almost everything; when time, distance and pace is one's Holy Trinity. I've come to love the days of now, when they are not.

When I coached at Oglethorpe, one of my best friends, Phil Wendel, re-introduced me to running. I was a tennis coach who'd gone a bit fat, couldn't run a mile without bending over and grabbing my knees. Phil and I went through heaven and hell together – the beginning and ending of relationships, the ups and downs of sports, the rollercoaster slings, arrows and roses of life. Through it all, he made me get out there.

I think God was my eye and ear witness the day that Indiana Hoosier grabbed this Georgia Redneck by the shirt sleeve and said, "As long as we are able – no matter what is going on – we will keep up our running."

I move forward believing in Phil's words, God, karma and kindness, and I have stayed true to that oath even when one day I wished it had killed me. I've written probably far too much of my Great Depression of 2006 and 2007, but I'm here to tell you, it's hard to run distance when you don't have your heart.

To this day – of all the miles I've logged – by far my toughest athletic accomplishment wasn't the marathons, but the day I ran Buzzard Bait at Smoky Mountain Running Camp a depressed man. I would say it was tough physically, mentally and spiritually, but I possessed no spirit.

I think it was the ghost of my father, the Good Lord, every angel at every disposal, Phil's promise – all hands-on deck – that led me across that finish line, drawn in the sand by another distance runners' foot.

In moving forward, today I'm told they are temporarily closing down the sacred river – a government shutdown. The bathrooms, gates, parking lots will be sealed off. I felt like I was being kicked out of there this morning by the powers that be.

Let's see, government shutdown. From people that can't get along. Political crap. Egos. Greed. The lust for power.

And that's supposed to keep me from running? Really?

My immediate thoughts went to a promise made to a great friend; my dad's eyes lighting up when he found out I was to be a runner; and the sheer beauty of getting outside and moving forward leads me to only one sane conclusion:

Tomorrow, if not sooner, I will lace up my shoes and I will run.

Peace, love and closed gates be darned…

A 'BULL DURHAM' PRE-RACE CONVERSATION

It's show time, go time – Saturday morning. The dew is rising off the ground while the sun is peeking down on it. The kids are stripped down, warmed up, ready to run. They stand in a huddle, about forty yards from the starting line.

Usually one to leave them alone, this time you approach. After all, what's the mood? Their thoughts? Race plans? Are they good and warmed up? Why is it so cold when it was 80 degrees yesterday? Why don't they have episodes of 'Scrubs' and 'Cheers' on anymore?

The huddle breaks and you walk in the center, poised, ready to deliver. But then:

"Coach Dunn, what's your spirit animal? Mine is either the chicken or the guinea fowl?" Berkley says this, though you're not really sure why. With the delivery, however, she breaks into a pose, and damn if she doesn't look exactly like a chicken.

After all, her hair is pointed upward, straight up, pointed, looks just like one. Her waist is off to one side while the rest of her torso is on the other. So, instead of breaking into 'Nick Saban's Greatest Hits' as far as pep talks, you laugh.

But wait! Her blue, beady eyes are staring at you, lifting, demanding your answer. You're not really sure why, but she REALLY wants to know what your spirit animal is.

"Well, I'm not sure if I have a spirit animal, but in college people often told me I reminded them of a puppy dog," you manage. "You know, my tail's always wagging and I'm always wanting to see and be seen."

Berkley's foot goes off to the left, her hand to her side, she looks up, considers, and then this: "That is SO you! That's hilarious!" The other girls chime in, point at you, one girl's hand goes over her mouth she's laughing so hard.

You turn red, though hopefully none of them will notice with your hat pulled over your eyes. You ponder, the brain spins, tries to get the subject back to – you know – this running thing.

"Well…."

"Sorry, Coach Dunn, we have to go race!"

And with that you're bombarded by seven sweat tops, three bracelets, two watches and a set of earrings.

So there you stand. Alone. A used clothes warehouse. Pep talk prepared but never delivered. Race strategy shuffled in your head but never dealt. The good coach who cares!

Oh well, what's a lonely puppy dog to do…

ADVENTURES AND MIS-ADVENTURES OF A CROSS COUNTRY ROAD TRIP

Pre-Race

"Do you think in German or in English? You're addressing one Aidan Zeissner – an internal lad if there ever was one – and he's walking to the vans, head down. He looks into you, probably questioning why you're making him talk but you have no way of knowing this.

"Mostly German," he says. If Aidan has eight words to spare, he'll give you two of them. Still, you smile, glad he's on this trip – this senior you've watched transfer from a decent runner to a Human Gazelle in the wink of an eye. You mumble something else about thinking in pictures instead of words, but Aidan just looks at you, smiles, the probable equivalent of "I've already spoken to you Coach Dunn. Now kindly get out of my way while I pack and get ready."

The girls are late – fashionably late – and they walk up all as one like they usually do. "We were going to text you, but we were standing…right there," Caroline Lyles says as she gestures off to a slew of trees about 20 yards or so away, as if this would make her point.

Remembering Caroline as a former shy girl herself, you simply accept the explanation and count yourself lucky to be collecting all these syllables so early in the day. The triplets – she, Erin Hill, and Jessica McNair – board in order – also as expected – and you feel a sense of normalcy in watching them do so.

These three – as freshmen – used to share the same lane during speedwork days. At running camp in

Asheville, all would sit in the same seat on the bus even though many other seats were open. You smiled then at seeing that and you smile at the thought now.

Silently, you hope they will all live to be 97, pass away on the same day, be buried in the same casket – holding hands of course – with music blaring out of Erin's speakers while the mourners file in.

Anyway, fourteen board bus #17 – getting said bus required not much short of ripping open a vein. Still, it is equipped with three quarters a tank of gas, way too wide mirrors, and a hard enough side frame that, if you lean back and fall asleep on it, your back and neck will be sore sometime up until the next eclipse.

They told you they wanted you going in one of the new buses – more dependable and safer you were told. Hold the phone on that comment. Hold the phone.

Anyway, Liam Hill, our hockey player, gets on next. You've told him the temperatures are expected to be somewhere between heat and overkill at race time. Hating warm weather with a passion times 12, his facial expression tells you he's ready to throw off the hockey gloves and push your face in just for telling him this.

In the end, though, he just drops his head and smiles, heads straight to the back, plops down.

Maddie Lowe is seated across the aisle to your left – she's fresh off of a wreck just yesterday but is and was too shy to tell anyone about it. (Where did we get all these shy people from?). "How did you know about that?" is her only question.

You tell her you're the carpool chief, you know all. Polite enough not to tell you you're an idiot, she just smiles and resumes her conversation with Ella Pappas.

It is Matthew Raeside who is the only one who has his

own seat. He is the "Rudy" movie that hasn't been written yet, though he'll never not only sack a Georgia Tech quarterback in his time, but none from any other team for that matter.

What he does is take his point of interest and stay with it more than persistently – like water hitting a rock – and before long you're staring out into a Grand Canyon he created and wonder just what the heck happened and when?

He started his high school running career as "The Kid Whose Name We'll Probably Never Learn" and is ending it as Captain Raeside. And you can believe those capital letters have been earned...

There have been times of late when you've watched him address the team, all listening in respect, and you can't help but get a tad weepy at the thought. Tom Hanks' voice – There's no crying in cross country!" – briefly pops into your head, but you dismiss it. After all, there IS crying in cross country, and anything else you have the guts to throw yourself into and love.

So instead of wiping away the tears, you simply dismiss the saying – alongside the other ones you hate like "absence makes the heart grow fonder" – and you move on.

One more word about the bus – Coach Susan Jones is the driver. She, like you, has a tennis resume – played at Florida State, coached it later, all that. Still, you remember three years ago when you suggested she accept the JV girls' tennis position at school. You've rarely seen her mad, but on that day, she glared at you – the way your mother used to do when you forgot to take out the trash – and went off to coach golf instead.

Golf, track, passing a kidney stone? Anything, just not tennis.

Suddenly you put the mind on shuffle, listen to the music coming out of Erin's speakers. Suddenly, the girls are all braiding each other's hair; the guys talking about everything and nothing. Suddenly, there's a rhythm forming to this life, this trip, this day.

And suddenly, you wonder why the van is only going 35 miles per hour down I-75, with angry drivers passing.

Something We Didn't Plan On

Somehow a guy with a Dent Magic t-shirt is standing outside our van, talking to Coach Jones. Somehow and from somewhere, a Monroe County policeman is there, too. You've made calls to everyone who will listen – your athletic director, his secretary, the head of security, the head of facilities, your co-head coach. You even called your brother and girlfriend, for the heck of it, just to say, "You ain't going believe this (bleep!)"

Messages are relayed, their people calling their people who texted their people who emailed theirs. Parents were informed, hold the presses, details coming soon.

Somehow, we're now at a gas station, the boys playing football, the girls only wanting to know if they can go to the bathroom. Mrs. Sapone appears in her car; Mr. Raeside soon behind in his truck. Equipment is transferred, moved around, shuffled, then some.

This seems chaotic yet organized somehow. Coach Jones' brother comes back in from Macon to snatch up four of us, five go with Mrs. Sapone, and somehow it has come to pass that you're driving a truck with four in tow down I-75 south.

You recall this last time you drove a truck; it was sometime around Jimmy Carter's presidency, and you can't help thinking how, in the old days, you'd have simply thrown each and every one of your kids back in the cab, driven on, and nobody would've known or cared.

Do that now, and you're soon looking at blue lights, hand cuffs, and jail. Oh my.

Race Time

The Honorable Susan Jones fired the ceremonial gun to start the girl's race. To your knowledge, she killed, wounded, or harmed no one with the shot, the race went off without a hitch, and all 113 girls – as far as you know – ran off in the right direction.

Her family was and is instrumental in this First Day Presbyterian place, donated, money, land, passion, and the works into helping this race, this course, and this school happen. She was going to come here without us – if she had hopefully, she wouldn't have broken down and might've gotten here a lot sooner.

Liam – the man who hates it when it gets above 50 degrees – ironically was the best runner in the pack on this day when it was 93 at gun shot. He ran a time he wasn't proud of, and an interview with him afterwards would've made Norman Vincent Peale turn over in his grave. It was "The Power of Negative Thinking" on steroids.

How was the course? Gravelly. How was your start? Slow. How were the conditions? Hot. How was the footing? Bad. How do you feel? Cramped.

It is also to be noted that our beloved Captain Raeside, overachiever and all, took ninth.

Leading the girls was Emily Kallis, who has logged

more miles than cross country kids in the last three years – despite not running cross country. She made her debut – broken vans, hot temperatures, firing guns and all – and took fifth overall. Maddie – car wreck yesterday be darned – was ninth.

The girls' team got second, posed with a trophy, smiled for all cameras, cell phones and real, adding equipment to this trip where we already have no place to put it.

Just thinking: Coach Jones and her gun. Liam and his win. The girls and their trophy. And may all mother's hearts be warmed at this, if only this: At the starting line – despite all – they looked so happy. Content. Bonding. At peace. You want your kid safe and happy? Well, the safe thing was a matter of question a couple hours ago. The happy? To quote from Chevy Chase, "it would take a plastic surgeon to get the smiles off their faces."

Finish Lines

Later. Invading Mellow Mushroom. Prepared to give the athletic credit card a hernia and then some. Party of 20, or 21. Who's counting?

It seems one of the girls has a little game she plays after practice. She goes around the room and asks everyone two questions: First, what was your popsicle? And second, what was your poopsicle? The popsicle being the best thing about the day; the poopsicle being about what...well...sucked.

The usual answers come out, the best being here in Macon, the worst having to study for a math quiz when they got home late. Like that. As for you, you've trained yourself only to think of the good things – this life thing being a gift you've done nothing to deserve.

So later, as the final credits of Two and Half Men roll and you stare off into your ceiling back home in the overbuilt city of Sandy Springs, you can't help but think this:

Your bus broke down at some exit called Johnsonville Road – middle of nowhere. Within what seemed like minutes, Mr. Dent Magic and a cop were there. After getting the van up to the gas station, again – in minutes – Mrs. Sapone and Mr. Raeside were there.

All in all, you arrived at the meet only about 40 to 45 minutes late. That's insanity how good and lucky that is and was! The Heavens sent angels from all directions, the second we said Ouch, if not before.

Your popsicle? You've landed at a great place; among the best people you've ever been around. You've landed at a school that possibly helped save your life. You just spent time with your team, another coach, and parents – all who contributed to what just happened.

Take one person out and we may've been screwed – or still on I-75 – or still on our cell phone asking for help and wondering why. Or maybe you'd be calling your girlfriend again, saying "This (bleep) is still happening!"

Your popsicle is just this: May you be here for as long as you possibly can. Every day is a pure moment – you want to be no place else. Every day you smile while girls braid each other's hair, boys try to flirt, coaches try to make sense of it all, and we all train despite the temperatures.

While all this goes on, there is support, angels, and the Heavens, looking on from every and all sides. Wrongs are righted, a GPS from the Gods sets us right in spite of ourselves, and reminds us to just relax, keep moving forward, we've got this!

A smile comes across your face – and how could it not – as you close your eyes and go to sleep.

Good night…

REMEMBERING BOSTON

When you get off the bus before the Boston Marathon, you can see a sign that reads: "Do you believe in hallowed ground? Yes, you are on it!"

Personally, I failed time and again before I ever qualified. In D.C., I made a bid only three days after a colonoscopy. The race ended with me walking the last half and cussing at a gummy bear. Unfortunately, I'm not kidding.

In Florida it was 75 degrees, so I ended up in a wheel chair; a nurse asking questions. I nailed the first two and then she ordered: Spell your last name. "(Bleep) it," I said. "Wheel me in."

She did…and proceeded to pump three IV bags into me. My non-running wife didn't understand. Why was I 30 pounds too light and doing this to myself? In retrospect, I see her point. Still, at the time, it was all about staying light, getting on a plane, running 26.2 miles, staring at my watch, repeat.

And praying the time would be 3:20 or less.

In Chicago, the time finally was, as I guess God got tired of my misery, my cussing, my training, my constantly getting on a scale because I just ate half of a half of a salad with almost a tomato on it. And don't forget that pickle.

On that day in the Windy City it was 39 degrees. No wind. Perfect conditions. My friend Phil ran the last 10 miles with me. He was funny like that – always in good enough shape to run double figure miles because he could help. Also, because he's a Hoosier and I'm yet to meet a bad one.

For once – and I'm still not sure how this happened – I

morphed into a smart runner - one who actually had a plan and stuck to it. I ran 7:35's the whole way, then did a 7:22 on Mile 26 just for fun – and because I could. I still have the picture, simply couldn't throw it away.

I write this because Boston comes around every April – ready or not, qualified or not - and sometimes our runners ask me about marathons. What it's like? Would you do it again? I never encourage a high school kid to run one – their legs are still developing. Run 10Ks, maybe a half-marathon, enter your local 5K. Hug a stranger, buy someone a cup of coffee.

But don't run a marathon. Not yet.

Still, I recall that night in Chicago – Boston ticket successfully punched – eating out. Phil told some surrounding people I had just qualified. The group immediately went silent, turned their chairs towards me, leaned in.

"How'd you train?"

Silence and shock were my answers. They were asking ME! And as a former reporter, I'm used to asking the questions…

How did I train? Would I do it again? On one hand, it cost me pain, injuries, colds, and a wife. It took money, flying which I hate, and claustrophobic chutes and starting lines. My back, to this day shoots me the proverbial bird when I put on my socks. And porta-johns before a marathon? Most disgusting thing ever – bar nothing. Even stink can't survive in those things.

But the goal setting! The discipline, the work, the bond. Did I say the bond? The stories I collected, the people I met, the cities I saw, the medical tents I borrowed, the weight I had so much fun later gaining back, the hugging the Wellesley girls at Mile 13.

Still, as for present day, I won't do it again – too much

time involved. I don't miss waking up at dark thirty and going on a long training run. It's brutal, thorough, involving.

Yet I smile...because I have done it all before...and because every April I can remember Boston.

And every April, I can remember one moment in time, when a pack of runners got quiet, leaned forward, and asked a smart runner-for-a-day how he trained...

MY LOVE TO THE BOSTON MARATHON

On this day when many are out running the Boston Marathon – I just want to crank out some memories:

- There is nothing more disgusting than a Porta-a-Jon before a marathon. Not sure which is worse, using one of those things or getting a biopsy for prostate cancer. If the doctor puts you to sleep, I'm picking the biopsy.

- It could be anywhere from 30 degrees and snowing to 80 degrees and humid. Flip your coin, book your flight, make your reservations, and pay your entry fee. Good luck!

- Cheers was great afterwards, but I wanted to sit between Norm and Coach at the bar. Didn't happen. And the barkeep looked nothing like Ted Danson or Woody Harrelson.

- They used to have a marathon party at some joint, complete with results posted at the door. Sorry, but there's not much funnier than watching people try to dance after running 26.2 miles. Picture bobble head dolls, partially paralyzed, and just out of the box.

- Heartbreak Hill, unless you're trying to qualify for the Olympic Trials, is overrated. It's a long, gradual hill that just happens to be in a bad place – in the latter miles.

- One year I wrote my name on my shirt. A rather non-sober gentlemen cussed at me and told me to "charge my (bleep) up that (bleeping) hill and now!" There were other nasties fired my way, but I was halfway up the hill before he finished.

- Running downhill for miles and miles is HELL on your thighs. It's the only course I ever ran where I was actually READY to start going uphill.

- Qualifying for this – way back in 2001 – was the highlight of my athletic career – and I was one who attempted almost every sport.

- Hearing other people's stories on the bus ride of how they qualified was worth the price of admission. I met a lady who qualified under the midnight sun, another who trained 100% on a treadmill because of bad weather. One didn't train at all. Latest report he's still on Mile 12.

- At the finish line in 2002, I burst into tears – still not sure why. It wasn't emotions, pain, or because I was sad. Maybe it was the only thing I had left in my body.

- It took me four marathons before I qualified. Still, it was worth it – a fascinating experience Mile 1 through Mile 26. It's that last .2 that almost killed me.

- I ran beside and had almost the exact same time

as my first college girlfriend – we were in the same starting coral. Funny thing is, I never saw her once. Maybe she hid, just like in the good ole days.

- Loved running past Fenway – GREAT ballpark. May the childhood memories of Carl Yastrzemski, Billy and Tony Conigliaro and company never die.

- Sitting in an airplane with a sore butt isn't and wasn't fun. You may think a Delta gin & tonic would ease the pain. You would be wrong.

- Bless you all who qualified and were trained and ready. I feel your pain – emotionally as well as physically. You are stronger because of it – you'll come back better this fall.

And as always, my love to New England, with or without Tom Brady.

A RUNNING FRIENDSHIP

I met the guy in Asheville, NC at this thing called running camp. He was my suite mate. I remember shaking hands with him – back in the day when you could do such things – standing between the couch and the hallway in Mills Hall, Room 301.

Little did I know that, within five years, our lives, souls, and careers would be joined at the hip.

I remember, also that week, hearing him speak of "getting on the podium" at the pacing contest. I'd never thought of anything in terms of podiums before – little did I know it would be a phrase that would stick, follow me back to Atlanta, off to tracks and cross country courses across the state.

We were two lost souls when we met, both floundering as far as work, trying to make it in a world where we'd been square pegs in round holes, too old or too young for jobs, too male, too tall, too short, too democratic, too republican.

God has a sense of humor, though, he put us in the same place, at the same school, co-coaching the same teams, even co-working carpool if you can believe that. Though I got here first, one of my happiest moments was getting him his job – the head of the religion department hired him sight unseen based on my words. I'm a flawed soul, but I speak and write from my heart. If I see truth, love, and light in you, I'll share it, flaunt it, brag on you at water coolers.

Our plans are to retire from Holy Innocents' when we're approximately 115 years old. Me, I want to be standing at the finish line in Carrollton, yellow note pad in hand, and simply keel over. Don't be sad, I'm a fortunate soul, a flawed but well-meaning lad.

As for him, he will be clapping his hands sideways the way he does, he'll die so proud of his runners, his program. One of his kids will outperform his Rain Man numbers and he, too, will conk out. We'll be buried exactly a 5K apart, the distance of cross country races.

We've been through a lot together. We've been ranked the best and came out not so much. We've stood at the top of his sacred podium. We've ridden buses at dark thirty on Saturday mornings, traded numbers and races and paces, talked about how fleet of feet our runners are or are not.

It's track season now and we'll freeze together this afternoon. He'll have on that goofy hat with a whistle around his neck. I'll be clad in 17 layers. Still, it's a good union, he and I. We love our kids. We love our school. And we've come to lean on each other, because we've both needed it.

Funny how things work. It constantly teaches me to do what you're supposed to do and then stay out of the way. Feel as good as you can, because that's what let's God in, and just go with it. Sorry, and no offense to the planners and goal setters out there, but my goal is happiness, and to share what I've learned and who I've learned it with.

And I've learned a lot through my friend in this picture. I've helped my friend in this picture. And he dang sure has helped me.

Here's to you Coach Jayaraj...and here's to a great week...

WHEN RUNNING SUCKS

Sometimes you just have to say it.

As one who has read about the joys of running, runners' high, peak performances, and while watching the 2016 Olympics and seeing the track athletes gliding through their lanes, there comes a time when you have to face the facts that sometimes – well actually often times – this sport is simply not always easy. In fact, it never is.

I remember it well. It was in my tennis days – 1992 – when I was the coach at nearby Oglethorpe University. The season had ended and I felt lost. After walking around and across the empty courts on the first afternoon that we would've normally been practicing, for whatever reason I ended up down at the track. I figured, I'm a big shot tennis guy; I can run a mile easily enough. Why not?

Now, as much as I'd love to report that the laps disappeared quickly behind my feet, my body was fluid as I made the curves, and my mind, body and spirit were all one as I completed my four-lap effort, I will not.

In fact, it happened this way: When I took the last agonizing step, after I crossed that SFL (sacred finish line), and while I was bent over with my hands on my knees and trying my best not to throw up my #1 with lemonade at Chick Fil-A, my lone thought was this: "Wow, that absolutely blew!"

In getting a bit off the subject (or maybe not), I had the same thoughts about my first attempt at meditation. As one who has read about the benefits of it for twenty-plus years, my first experience with it this past March yielded similar if not the same results.

I expected to get up from my seat with flutes playing

in my brain and visions of sitting next to God. Instead I got up, turned off my timer and thought to myself, "Well, that absolutely blew!"

But perhaps I digress.

This tale actually begins when I was living in Florida, disguised as a married man, but with my only real passion shaving precious seconds off my 5K time, standing on some random podium with a medal wrapped around my neck and reading my name in next morning's *Palm Beach Post*. (Actually, I wrote for the *Post*, so that was the easy part.)

As for my life at the time - even as a forty-plus year old - I still had some of the frustrations of staring at a blank line on my resume that said, "OBJECTIVE:" This scared me – often it still does – but my Florida years helped me work that out. I now have it narrowed down to a wonderful simplicity now – I like to read, write and run. Quite frankly, anything else is kind of a distraction.

So now I'm in Florida and I'm running. It's the last tenth of a 5K and I'm sprinting for my life. Not blessed with speed, strength or a kick, bless my heart I ran and raced hard and this day was no exception.

There was a man kicking it in right next to me – a pious, righteous soul. I know this because he was yelling, "Praise Jesus. Praise the Lord!"

Me, I've been diagnosed with a bit of Tourette's syndrome, so if I'm running along and my thoughts are, "I feel like (bleep)," then what comes out of my mouth is, "I feel like (bleep)."

Anyway, we're closing in on the finish line – he's praising Jesus, Mary and all available angels and saints and I – well – had different things escaping my mouth.

"Yes Lord, I'm running to please You. I'm running because of your Glory oh God," said he.

And I said: (Bleep), ouch, this is hurting like (bleep); I feel like (bleep); (bleep) this and (bleep) that. (Bleep), (bleep) and (bleep). And one more (bleep) just for the (bleeping) (bleep) of it!

You get the point. Anyway, we crossed the finish line and I had to find him. Being a generally sweet soul (in spite of my mouth), I like to leave things good with people if at all possible. If somebody has a bad day, I don't want it to be on me.

I found him at the tables between the Gatorade and the bagels. He had a towel wrapped round his neck and he was looking for people to mingle with, talk about the race, share times and swap stories.

"Hey, there you are!" When I approached, his eyes became lasers; they were angry, piercing and closing with every stride I took towards him. I knew I had to talk quickly so I did. "Between me and you, we just had Heaven and hell completely covered just then, didn't we?"

I laughed.

He did not. In fact, if he had run as fast during the race as he did to get away from me, he would've broken the tape.

Let's move forward, shall we?

I was running at the river the other day – the river is a beautiful, peaceful, scenic place if there ever was one, and on this fine Sunday there were hundreds of us out there beating the heat that was later to befall us. I had just returned from Nike camp, so I was all decorated in my "Just do it" attire – could've perhaps played a part in one of their commercials.

The dress was perfect, but the run was not. My mind was a cesspool times twelve. To share a quick part of it, it went something like this:

> *Good God I've got to make a dentist appointment and school's about to start and I've got a hundred cross country kids to look after and I haven't moved in to my office yet and my laundry is starting to smell like crap and I've got to get the oil changed in my car, and when is pay day anyway because I've got to pay that housekeeper and my home owners and …*

I won't go on. After all, I don't want to be noted for having the longest run-on sentence in the history of modern day journalism. Still, I eventually finished the five-mile course I had mapped out, crossed the SFL walked to the bench to do my stretches and I thought to myself, "Well, that certainly sucked!"

I asked our counselor at my school about this – that river run on that day. I sat on her couch – of course there's a couch – and she took off her glasses after hearing my story, wiped her brow, stared me straight in the eyes.

"Let me see if I've got the facts right," she began. "It's a perfectly nice weekend – you could've gone to bed on Saturday, set the alarm for Monday, and skipped the whole day if you'd wanted. Instead you got up at in the wee hours on Sunday, you ran five miles in ninety degree heat, alone, through the woods and the mud and the rocks, probably surrounded by snakes, and the whole time you internally yelled at yourself. Do I have this right?"

My face was red as a brick but I didn't want to lie. "That is correct."

She re-wiped her brow, put her glasses back on.

"So what's my verdict," I impatiently asked.

She didn't hesitate. "You're a wack job! All you runners are!"

There I sat all red and all guilty and all ...

"But at least hear this," she continued before I got out the door. "At least you got the thoughts out. I mean, if it weren't for the run, all that internal mess would still be in there. In your own demented way, you've gone a long way towards quieting your demons. I'll give you, and all you runners that much credit anyway."

So there you have it. I'm hearing an evangelist in my head right now as I write this from some 80s movie yelling, "I have exorcised the demons!" Maybe that, all alone, is enough. Game. Set. Match.

Her words and my own experiences lead me to this and this only: There's no such thing as a bad run...or a bad meditation for that matter. The only bad ones are the ones you don't show up for.

So keep moving forward.

Bleep, bleep...

GOD RUNS THE PEACHTREE ROAD RACE

Hey God, will you run the Peachtree Road Race with me next week?

No, I most certainly will not.

Why not?

I don't have a number.

You mean God has to have a number before he can run the Peachtree?

Of course, the Atlanta Track Club has made that very clear. I'm surprised you didn't know this after all these years. After all, the race has been going on since 1970.

That's actually accurate, I think.

It is according to an old article that appeared in the *Northside Neighbor* one summer. It said that the race started in 1970 with 110 runners and that Jeff Galloway, who went on to be an Olympian in 1972, won the race. He ran in Munich with your other hero, Steve Prefontaine.

Hey, I wrote that article!

Oh dear, never mind. It's probably not accurate in that case. Just forget I said anything.

Do I get points for being close? Anyway, come run with me! I'd love to have God at my side while we cruise down Peachtree Street toward downtown Atlanta! Still, I must warn you—there's a lot of drinking and carrying on that goes on along the streets as we run down. Just sayin'.

I don't want to get in trouble for running as a bandit. Being God and all, I have to sort of set the example.

I don't think the Atlanta Track Club will have you arrested; they'll have more pressing matters on race day. I should've shot you a notice when I signed up in March when the entries came out in the local paper, but of course, I forgot.

That's right, you were away on your little sabbatical, though from what you were escaping I'm not sure. It's okay, though; I might not have heard you anyway. I'm busy in March with every college basketball fan and player sending me signs, shooting their fists at me, and begging me to help them throw that silly orange ball through the hoop. You humans really are amazing.

I'm starting to think you have an issue with basketball.

Not with the game, but what is it with you people and deadlines? I mean, why does March Madness not end until April? What's up with that? And do you realize that right now it's late June and the NBA just got finished earlier this week?

Who won?

Who cares? It's late June! People are vacationing! Something about watching an NBA game while sitting poolside or at the beach just doesn't go together. And it shouldn't! What is it about timetables you people don't understand?

I'm even thinking about sending down this memo I just finished writing:

> **After the taxes are done on April 15, I will *not*—I repeat, will *not*—be taking any more basketball requests. Turn in your uniforms and go play something warm. For any questions or concerns, my basketball office will reopen this October 1, and not a day before. Have a nice day.**
>
> **Love always,**
> **God**

I like your writing style, God. You are very straight and to the point. I wish you would've written some of those books I had to read in high school. It seems writers back in the day actually got paid by the word and man did it ever show!

Leave writers alone! Most of them have suffered quite enough! And look who I'm telling!

Good point, but can we get back to running the Peachtree?

Sure, what do you want to know?

I think it'd be a hoot and a half if you'd run it with me. I'm curious; what kind of pace does God run? What kind of shoes? Are you a Nike man? How about Asics, New Balance, Brooks, Mizuno—which one? Besides, with you at my side, I feel we could win it!

Not a chance! Even God can't run as fast as the Kenyans no matter what kind of shoes I wear. Simply can't be done.

Interesting—even God can't run a sub-thirty-minute 10K. Now I don't feel so bad.

I don't think my 10K personal record is anything anyone should be concerned with. As I've said many times, no one cares about stuff like that except for you. Now what's your issue with the Peachtree?

I'm just not sure I want to run it by myself.

Did you say by yourself? There are going to be, like, sixty thousand people out there; well more than that if you count the bandits and the crowd! What exactly is alone about that?

Wow, even God says "like"; boy, the high school kids are going to love this! You know what I mean, though; I'd like to have someone keeping pace with me, maybe reading me my splits and telling me to speed up or slow down.

I promise you I'll send down all kinds of characters you can run with. There will be one or two dressed like Uncle Sam and many with their faces and bodies painted the sacred red, white, and blue. It will be sensory overload, as

you like to say. I'll even send a group that you can relate to - they will be running as a six-pack. They will even have a little six-pack ring around all of them, so you should feel right at home!

Thanks again, I think.

Once again, I say—and once again you won't believe me—I will never leave you alone. And as for my advice: watch out for mile five.

You mean mile four; that's Cardiac Hill.

And that's precisely why I'm telling you to watch out for mile five! You see, everybody knows what Cardiac Hill is—most do, anyway. People get geared up for it, their adrenaline is pumping, and—for the most part—they do a better-than-ample job of getting up it. The problem is, there is a small hill on mile five; that's the one that gets a lot of people.

Why?

Because runners make the mistake of letting their guard down after getting up the big hill on mile four! Don't do that! Stay pumped up; you can relax toward the end. Look at the course as a miniature replica of the Boston Marathon. Perhaps that will help you.

How?

Okay, tell the readers what happened to you the first time you ran Boston.

I was so excited to have finally qualified, to have finally gotten there! I think I peed myself more than twice!

Ahem. Even God doesn't want to know about that, and I consider myself a *very* open-minded God.

Sorry. As for the race, I rocked it—ran a PR even.

Great, now quit bragging and tell them what I'm asking for.

Well, most of the first half—if not all of it—is downhill, and then you start back up. Sort of like the Peachtree, as you said. That part was okay, and then I cruised up Heartbreak Hill! Why, I didn't even know that's what it was until I got to the top of it. I asked the runner next to me if that was it, and he let out a cussing streak a mile long. The gist of what he said was, yes, that was Heartbreak Hill.

Continue; what happened after that?

I relaxed—planned on cruising through the last five miles.

And? You're still avoiding the issue.

Then when I hit the hills on the last few miles, they dang near killed me!

Because you'd relaxed; your guard was down. You weren't mentally prepared. That's why I'm telling you what I'm telling you. You let out your own Tourette's

streak as you plodded up the hills on Miles twenty-two through twenty-six. You offended more than one man, woman, and child I might add.

Sorry about that.

I'm not the one to tell, but it's already forgotten. Just remember that this time—on mile five.

Anything else?

Don't forget your MARTA pass, though you might want to wait a little bit before getting on a train.

Why is that?

Why? Thousands of runners packed like sardines after running on a hot summer's day in July in one car, and you're asking why? Do you remember what your dad's socks smelled like?

That bad, huh?

No, nothing's that bad. Still, you might want to wait a while. Either that or take a taxi back up.

Where should I park my car?

In Atlanta? On a holiday? Parking in that city is bad enough on a regular Monday through Friday. How do you expect me to know where to park on a major holiday with a million people around?

Okay, okay; Brookhaven it is!

While we're at it, watch your diet not just the night before but also the week before!

What's wrong with my diet?

I'm sorry, but the four major food groups are *not* beer, candy bars, pizza, and chips and salsa! This does not work!

It got me through high school and college.

How old were you then? How old did you say you were now? How old would you like to grow to be?

Okay. Diet: check. Parking: check. Marta pass: check. Mile five: check. How about sleeping arrangements? I've often crashed at a friend's house closer to the course just so I can sleep in a little more. The problem is, I can never sleep the night before, and I can rarely sleep in a strange bed. What's the big word from God on this?

They say the best night for good sleep is two nights before the race, though I'm still not really sure who "they" are. As for sleeping in a strange house, pack your pillowcase.

Did you say pillowcase? What on earth for?

Because it smells like your sleeping arrangements at home and it's easy to pack! You don't need to bring your whole bed over—this would prove heavy, hard to

carry, and perhaps rude. I'm actually laughing as I picture your skinny self toting your entire bed into someone else's home. Pretty funny!

Duh!

Just bring your pillowcase and put it over the pillow. The smell will remind you of home, hence better sleep.

God, that almost makes good sense!

As you would say, thanks, I think.

It's too bad you won't run it with me. I was looking forward to having your company. Still, I can understand you shying away and everything. I mean, not being able to run a sub-thirty-minute 10K, and also, why would God want to get beat by a 61-year-old man? Just so you know, I completely understand.

Hold the phone; I'll be right back.

Are you leaving me?

Yes, for the first time ever, I am temporarily leaving you!

Why? Wait. Come back! Where are you going? You just said you'd never leave me and I'd never be alone! Wait!

I'm trying to buy a number, but the man won't do Venmo.

God has Venmo?

Yes, and this man won't honor it!

Jesus wept.

I'll tell him. And I'm getting a little upset myself. After all, another Peachtree is about to go down and I don't have a number!

Cheer up! I'll let you have my T-shirt if you promise to forgive me for most of my sins.

Is the Peachtree Road Race t-shirt really worth that much?

You'd be surprised…even God himself would be surprised…

CROSS COUNTRY RITUALS

Their ritual is always the same:

The last day our cross country team goes to the river before 'race day Saturday', the girls veer off the beaten path and go in the opposite direction of the rest of the pack. Instead of the 3-mile trail that was once rated by *Runner's World* as one of the best in the nation, they head backwards.

Moving through the parking lot, they go up the ramp we'd just driven down and take a left to go over the bridge. The scenery at this point gets interesting – if you look right while heading this route you see the hustle and bustle of the big city – an access road with I-285 behind it; bumper to bumper cars; the sound of horns, brakes, even car radios.

If you look left, however, you take in the tranquility of the Chattahoochee – the calm, flowing waters; ducks floating about; kayaks and rafts easily cruising through the day. Often, I laugh while making this run, as my mood can change simply by which direction I choose to face. Thankfully – and happily – most days I choose the river and I'd like to think my days pass easier because of it.

Back to the girls: they cross the bridge and go left into the secondary parking lot. There are bathrooms over there, picnic tables, plenty of extra parking spaces for those that couldn't fit on the "main drag" and – if you keep going far enough – another trail goes off into the woods.

I'm not familiar with the exact tree the girls run to, but they have one. And off that tree each girl picks a leaf.

"Everybody gets one," one of our top runners later

told me. "You hold on to your leaf and then, when you're running back across the bridge, you have to stop, make a wish and then throw your leaf into the river. If you see your leaf all the way down into the water, your wish will come true. If you don't, it won't."

In summation, I have no idea how these girls came up with this, though I have long held a respectful opinion of the spontaneity and the creativeness of the teenage mind. In my opinion, many adults make the horrible mistake of "trying to figure it out." Don't do this, I say. Simply observe and enjoy.

After all, they are fresher from God than we are. Their lives are busy – day in and day out it's a hustle. If they chose this ritual, then bless them. As for me, I often laugh to myself just picturing this – eight varsity runners standing and leaning over the bridge – some practically falling over and into the water. Each following their leaf as it swings with the wind, arcing and twisting and turning. Each set of eyes following their own – secretly hoping their wish comes true whether it be a prom date, an 'A' grade in APHUG, a better relationship with their parents, or a new car on their upcoming birthday.

On this day, my top seven and the alternate trot back onto the "normal" side of the river – their workouts done and over with. I can practically hear them before I see them – Megan Roddenbery is telling a story about the perils of senior portraits and all it stands for. The other seven line up straight across in listening, even though they've often been told to go two-by-two.

They hear, they understand, but a good story is a good story – all are looking at their co-captain while she explains how she screwed up a perfectly good picture and boy won't mom be appalled!

It's adorable. It's almost as if what happens to them has never happened before or never will again. Hence, the long line of listeners, the rapt attention, the continuous breaking of the two-by-two rule.

They circle around me as they get back, out of habit already starting to stretch. I almost ask them about their leaves but I don't. I don't because I understand their resilience – whether their leaf got hurled back onto the bridge or whether they saw it down or not, they are already off to other things, more adventures.

The leaf dropping was so five minutes ago – a lifetime in adult world. Instead I just remain silent, watch them stretch, listen to them giggle.

After all, another river run is scheduled soon, on another day after school. Things are normal – whatever that means --- as eight more leaves will soon curl, fly and lift through the air. Eight girls will bend over and stare down – their lives oh so temporarily depending on the result.

My job is simply to enjoy and live for this. And as my dad used to say, keep it coming...

I SHALL GATHER AT THE RIVER

Everybody needs their own personal haven. Everybody – no exceptions – particularly nowadays and following the pandemic.

We live in a time where the world is getting both better and worse at the same time – if that makes any sense. Turning on the news is a judgment call; I'm often okay with not knowing though I'm sure I'll catch flack for that. We have gunmen at concerts, shootings in hallways, democrats vs. republicans – even rappers often settle things with gun fire.

As for me, I have my running at the Chattahoochee River. Sometimes it's the only place that makes any sense. People go there to better themselves – almost all of them. Walkers, joggers, bird watchers, all ages, shapes and sizes. It's a positive place, the only thing I lose there are pounds off my waist.

One day in my 20-plus years there – and as a writer I always appreciate ironies – I saw two people yelling at each other. Remembering the times I was told to "take it outside" as a kid, I couldn't resist telling those two to "take it inside." They got mad at me. I didn't care then and I still don't now.

We don't yell at the river. We walk, talk, run, sweat, communicate. Wear your iPods if you want but you're missing out. There's the tranquility of the Chattahoochee on your right as you start out, woods on your left. You can hear nature and the sounds of people getting their groove on. News be damned – it can wait, at least for now.

On the best of days, you'll catch a deer or two trotting across the trail. Often, they will just chew on the grass and stare as you go by. And, if you're into a faster pace, the occasional snake will dart out.

It works for me, because the deer make me slow down while the snakes make me immediately break into speed work mode.

In moving on, I once wrote that my Sunday morning runs are my church. Many don't understand this, but it is what it is. You find your peace when and where you find your peace – particularly in this day and time.

Once, while under the influence of a spiritual video, I was asked to simply write down what makes me feel good. It didn't have to be anything huge – like hitting the walk-off grand slam or hurling the no-hitter. It could be as small as a 22-second conversation with a kid between classes, finding a quarter outside of Cracker Barrel, laughing at a Netflix episode of 'Community'. You get the idea.

The first thing I wrote: Sunday long runs at the Chattahoochee River.

In closing, I'm in class while I write this – have been assigned to the moods and angst of twenty 14-year-olds in English. They are energetic – words are flying out of their mouths at 120-miles per hour with gusts up to 250. It can take you out of your game, if you let it.

In my years on this planet, I've read and taught myself that you have to stop bad thoughts, otherwise they gain momentum and soon you're in a crap storm. It is at this time where I refer to my list – I keep it handy and I can't recommend that enough.

And there it is, perched among the top of the list is running at the river.

RUNNING CAMP? WHAT IN THE HELL IS THAT?

In three weeks, I'm off to running camp in Asheville, NC. The first time I told one of my students I was doing this, he quickly replied, "Running and camp are two words that should NEVER be used in the same sentence."

Another common response: "You're going to what? Running? Camp?"

That's what I thought. Still, I'm weird – so in 2004 – while still disguised as a married man, I signed up. In retrospect, the wife might have helped me out of the house, but that's another story. Still, I made the LONG drive from West Palm to Asheville. Spent a week up there.

Haven't been the same since.

Distance runners – I have found – are a different breed. It's a group where the pain and suffering creates a thick bond – makes you friends. It's kind of like, "Wow, you're as demented as I am! What's your name?" Yeah, something like that.

In Asheville, I enter every summer a time warp. Hundreds of us simply call a time out on life – I recommend this – and we head up into the mountains. We actually run up one on Friday – it's called Buzzard Bait. I remember trying to impress my peers at the starting line on that 2004 day.

"I feel like a million bucks," I said. My friend laughed. "That's great," he said. "Problem is, it takes three million to get to the top."

He was right. Damn him.

I commiserated my divorce in Asheville; found out I did and didn't have prostate cancer. My roommate last summer learned his wife was pregnant. (He flew out the third story window upon hearing the news, but also, another story.) I've coached my kids to first and last place finishes in the pacing contest. Came close to getting struck by lightning and dying there.

It's an adventure on steroids – where the very people that work you up are the same ones that help you through it. Strange, but there it is…

As for Asheville, it's the Berkeley of the South – a place where locals, hippies and tourists all share the same soil. Somehow, it all works. You can find anything up there – except a parking place – and the music and the food and the beer – and the people I've met – are priceless.

We go there to share this thing called distance running. Fifteen of my kids will be with me this July. I'm an observer of the game – I like to watch and hear them as they go through the week. It's a rollercoaster for them, though the mood swings will often be cured by one of the mountain trail runs.

I write this because camp of any kind keeps you young; gives you a time out you deserve. We're pounded with info and jobs and chores and information and comparisons. Mental health is a serious issue.

Me, I'm a selfish soul – probably take more "me" time than I should. I'm an experienced camp goer; twenty years ago, I went to an eight-week camp in New Hampshire. All I wanted was a part-time job; I came home with a wife. I looked on the sign-up sheet when I got home and didn't find a word on there about that anywhere. Still, I digress once again.

I'm ready for my time out and to move forward, though I know how weird that sounds. And perhaps as I pen these words, my own mental health should be called to question. After all, in three weeks I'm going to run up a mountain.

And I can't wait to do it.

THE MATURATION OF A RUNNER

When it comes to runners, we're all wacked. It's okay though, it's just a life sentence we must learn to live with. Case in point - the loudest scream I've ever heard came in the middle of a workout when my partner, upon looking at her watch, saw the numbers 0:00.00.

Perhaps you've been there, forgetting to start the watch when you're a driven person can be a rather tragic thing. For those of you who are caring, she eventually got over it – not much therapy required.

Moving on, in interviewing runners and being an avid participant myself, I found it hard to put us all in numerical stages. We're all in this cosmic dance with our own talents and mindset, so who's to say? Still, I had time on my hands, was bored, so I decided to do it anyway. Agree or disagree, please read on regarding the five stages of running.

Stage 1

So you want to be a runner? Actually you're not really sure but you've noticed how fit, skinny and angular runners all seem to be – all of them are angles and elbows, and that looks somewhat inviting to you. They all talk funny – mostly in numbers – but they seem to have this bond thing going…

So up you go, off to the running store to finance a pair of shoes and, after sleeping the best you could in nervous participation, you rose up from your bed in preparation to become a verb.

Face it; it's not good at first. Your legs are sore, you

make up excuses NOT to do it – alternatives such as 're-arranging your sock drawer', or 'taking a nap until the feeling goes away.' You realize, at this stage, that even one lap around a track is a LOT longer than it appears with the naked eye.

You both cuss and pray a lot at this stage, though it mixes in perfectly with how loud you're panting and breathing and panting some more.

Still, some quit at this point and Stage 1 was all you had. No apologies necessary. We live in an active world – yoga classes, swimming pools, tennis courts are all over the place – so there are other ways of getting fit. We bid you goodbye and with no hard feelings. After all, you are hereby certifiably sane.

You tried God Bless

Some of you, however, move on to:

Stage 2

You love this sport! In fact, Time, Distance and Pace are your Holy Trinity. Not only do you enter races, but you're also trying to break 22 in the 5K or break 21 or…face it, you're at the stage where you're always trying to *break* things!

When you're not running, you go to the bookstore and buy a running log to chart your mileage. You subscribe to magazines; you buy GPS watches; you dream of PRs when you're supposed to be doing other things.

When your favorite cheerleader is out practicing, you're in good enough shape to circle around her again and again until she notices you. On a good day, maybe she will wink.

See? Even flirting becomes easier when you're a fit runner. Stage 2 forever you say! Halleluiah!

Looking at the whole picture, you do have a life, but your mood depends on the results of your next race – which is coming very soon! Always very soon…I should know; I was once a pretty good, Stage 2 runner. It cost me a wife, a microwave and my favorite dog, but by gosh I was a good runner!

Stage 2 is a great stage – one people want to remain in forever. Good for you if you can accomplish this (please let me know how), but for the rest of us, eventually gravity, an injury or two, and/or kinks in our joints do set in. Which leads us to:

Stage 3

One day before a run, you actually decide to NOT turn on your watch. You wonder if this will anger the Gods; you perhaps call yourself names, even feel a tad guilty. You wonder if lightning will strike you dead – on the spot.

But wait, your PRs are behind you! You now race a little less and you just want to see if you can run – gasp – for the fun of it. Is this actually legal? Do you change sports where you can keep getting better instead of sticking to one where you're getting worse? I quit tennis for this VERY reason.

To compensate for this, you still set your weekly mileage goals. After all, you've got one foot still in PR-land and another in "aging gracefully." You set a number, you learn to live with or without the watch, and off you go.

In looking at it, this is a strange stage. After all, what do you put down for pace in the log books? And you really don't want to run with Apps, because they announce it loud, real loud, where not only you but others can hear it!

The comparisons in your head can make this terribly embarrassing.

This is simply not acceptable. Cheer up, though – there are plenty more good miles ahead which leads to:

Stage 4

Run when you can, to stay in shape and simply for your health. Yes, you may find yourself running less in this stage but guess what? Every run is more sacred! After all, you're not forcing anything. Sometimes you line up for a run and don't even know (or care) how many miles you're going. This is also called the "Smell the Roses" stage where you run for enjoyment, you run because you can, you run because life is good. Once, in fact, you got lost from your pre-determined 5-mile trail run, zigged instead of zagged, therefore making it a little longer. Or a little shorter.

And what did you record later in your book? Who the hell cares! Nobody!

Let's move on now to Stage 5 now, shall we?

Stage 5

Stage 5 is the same as stage 4 except sometimes – if we're lucky to live long enough – we may replace some (or all) of your runs with walks. No watch, no worries, no pace, no problem. This is also a great stage because, if you do look at your watch halfway through only to see 00:00 on it, therapy will no longer be required.

You just smile; and you just keep going.

In summary, enjoy your stages I say, create your own even. Lie to yourself and say you're still running PRs when you're 64. Who cares? Run backwards if you want to, boxers have been known to do that when training for an aggressive opponent.

The trick, as always, is lacing them up and getting your butt out the door. After that, the rest comes naturally.

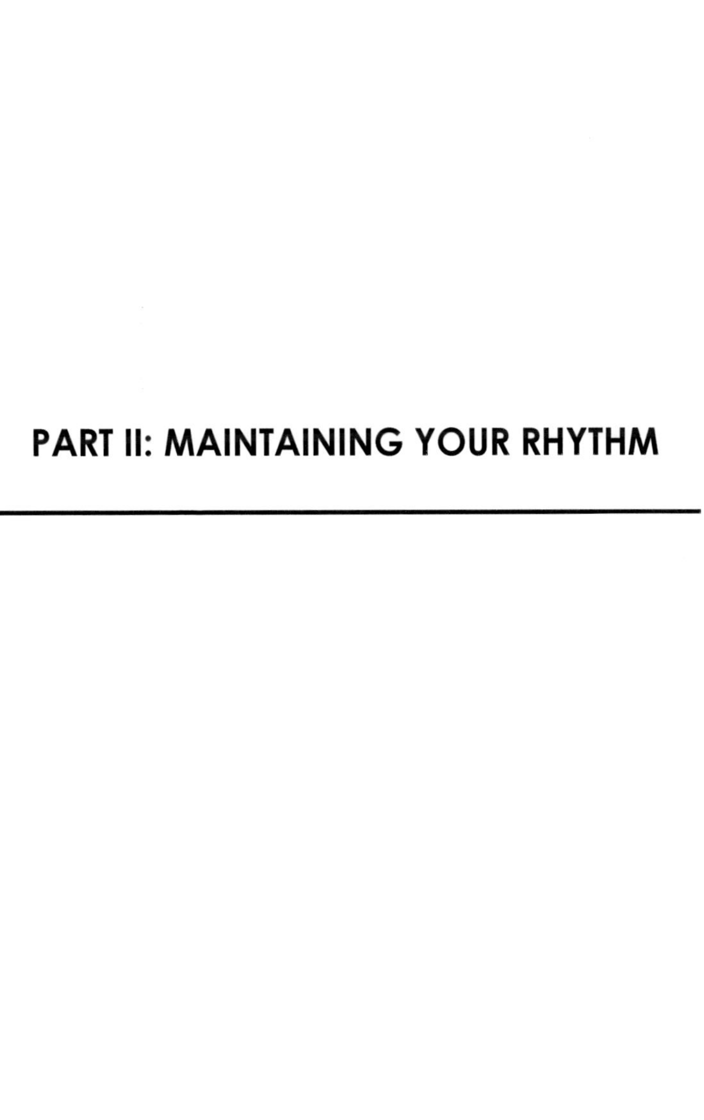

PART II: MAINTAINING YOUR RHYTHM

BREAKING BARRIERS...

"I want to break the five-minute mile."

It was one of our seniors, three days before cross country Senior Night. All teams do it differently, but we have a mile time trial a week before region. The idea is to get the fast twitch muscles going while keeping race sharp. Okay, maybe this makes us the Nick Saban of cross country coaches, maybe it doesn't.

Still, it's what we do. And a senior was taking it – not as a day to jog four laps and collect his goodie bag – but for real. A thing. A goal.

We'd been to the river the day before – or what I call the one-stop training shop. There are hills, marked quarters, flatlands, name your workout, it's all there, complete with bathrooms, water fountains, parking lots for stretching. When we got back, though, I watched while our senior walked to the track.

Watched him further while he stared at his watch, did a 100-meter stride, walked back, repeated the process. "What are you doing?" I asked, more curious as a writer than a coach.

"Visualizing," he said. "I'm getting the fourth lap inside my head. Every bit of it."

Ah, nice, I thought. At this point, I temporarily resigned as his coach and became his fan, his chronicler, a curious observer. "Just try to get some sleep tonight," I offered. "I will," he said, but we both knew he wouldn't.

Fast forward to race day: It was hot, too hot, 82 degrees in the shade. With his prior best time around 5:04, I didn't know if he could do it.

And, as unluck would have it – he went out too fast.

Way too fast – came in at the first quarter at 71. The coach in me was thinking, "Too hot, too fast, has never broke the barrier before. Las Vegas odds say he doesn't make it."

At the halfway point, he was at 2:30, dead on but still, two more laps. The heart dropped, though I remembered that mile records are run in negative splits, not positive like the 800. But still…

Then, it happened. The bleachers came alive. Our school is small. When Johnny breaks up with Sally in the morning, everyone knows by lunch. And when Blake wants to break five and had days to draw a crowd, people are THERE!

And forward they came. Beside me. At the finish line. "Let's go, Blake! Come on, you've got this!" But, in my mind, he hadn't, as after Lap 3 he was at 3:48, three seconds slow. Also, please remember, it was hot, he'd gone out too fast.

"I still had confidence," he said later. "I knew that I could do it."

Now, get the picture: Screaming teenagers. Nervous coaches. People staring at watches. Even the timer had a smile on his face.

With 300 meters to go, he started his kick. "Oh no," I thought. "There's too much track left."

But there wasn't. Picking up his stride, he was smooth with 200 to go, still gliding through the heat at 150. The clock, though, look at the damn clock…those numbers that seemed to be ticking off two seconds at a time.

I didn't look at my watch during his last 100, still don't regret it. After all, this was one of the many things that are so good about this sport. I mean, look at all these screaming people! I've heard less noise at crime scenes, car accidents, parades. I love this!

Seventy meters to go, 40, Blake is nothing but angles and elbows and knees and arms and legs and hair. His face looks like he's passing a kidney stone. If a wall were in front of him, I'd have bet on him even though he only weighed a buck-30.

He crossed the finish line and he screamed. Loud. Speaking of murder scenes, it sounded as if he'd just taken a bullet. Now, nervous or no, I looked at the time: 4:57. He dropped a 69 or so on the last quarter. In the heat. After going out too fast.

I shifted now from coach/journalist to observer. At this. These people. That clock. Blake. That look on his face. The fist pump in the air. Classmates congratulating him. Smiles – I could see where he used to have braces on his teeth.

Remembering to do my job, I recorded his time next to his name on my time sheet. Looking back over my shoulder as I moved away, I gave the whole scene one last look. At this sport. This race. This day. This sport we've chosen or that somehow chose us.

With nothing else left to do, I tucked the notebook under my arm and walked off the track…

HAPPY BIRTHDAY TO A GIRL FROM NEW JERSEY

This is perhaps a random column for Georgia folks, but I want to use this space to say Happy Birthday two days early to Madison Holleran, a two-sport star from up north who took her own life on Jan. 17th, 2014, while a freshman at U. Penn.

For some reason, this reminds me of a Facebook meme that went out a few years ago, talking about how - even if we did 99% of our job, thousands of New York Times papers wouldn't get delivered. The point was to stress that even an A-plus isn't good enough, and that we must be GREAT, we must be the BEST.

I call bullcrap on this, because I feel this pressure to be 100% all the time keeps us from taking a stab at things, giving something a try, getting out of our comfort zone. As I've written, I hate it when people use the term 110%.

Be your best, but on many days, you don't even get 90% - some days you're lucky to get 74. Every day is not a PR on the cross country course, every day is not an A-plus on the exam.

We push people too hard these days and at too young an age. I didn't know Madison Holleran, but I know she came up in this era of good, better, best, bigger, higher, faster. From what I've read, she was a beautiful, driven girl who did NOT get the better, better, best thing from her parents, but from this society we live in.

Comparisons – damn them to hell. Your best changes from day to day. Your fastest at times can be rather slow, your highest rather low. Sometimes it's okay to not be okay, and it's hard to get back on the proverbial horse when you're still in midair from falling.

Being in midair? That's okay, too, because as we've learned during COVID, there are times we must be off the ground where the earth can shift below us. Besides, it's been written that even angels don't sing all the time – so how and why should we be able to?

As a coach and as a human, the only pushing you'll ever get out of me is to be yourself. Copying anyone else is only getting half the final product – as no two are alike. Wake up, look up, try to cheer up. Be the best you can be on that particular day, and if thousands of people don't get their paper that day, that's just too bad. Go on-line. You don't need to be reading all that crap anyway.

So, Happy Birthday Madison Holleran. I never met you once, but I wish I did. And I love you for who you were, what you meant, and how you went about things.

And RIP to you and your dad. Together again, and at 100% without even trying.

PHOTOS WHERE I CAN FINISH

Running for me in my older days is the mental equivalent of taking out the trash, and while my younger goals consisted of slam dunking in the NBA or hitting forehand passing shots down the line at Wimbledon, later in life the aim is simply to be happy.

Period.

I've never been a believer in 'location, location, location,' simply because they only have a third of it right. Instead I go to 'location, chemistry, and timing,' my evidence being my most depressed time came while three-tenths of a mile from the ocean, 20 feet or so from a hot tub, surrounded by Florida palm trees, and only a mile or so from the nearest tekke bar.

Funny the things you remember – at my lowest of the low – it was the love of my dog – the one who used to lift up his back leg only to pee all over his front one – who brought me to my first return-to-sanity step when he quit sniffing the Sunshine State long enough to hop up on my leg in concern.

From this, I nurture my mental health more than a doting grandmother over her newborn, so much so that my screensaver – daily – reflects nothing but miles of smiles, races, faces, and paces - things that pull me forward.

I have learned: Write down what makes you happy. Surround yourself with photos, notes, happy emails. I even have a "gloat file" on my computer where I've saved the nice things people have written.

Still, it's the screensaver thing – especially since I'm

often staring at it when the mind won't settle and the words won't come.

There they are – my girlfriend Sheryl and I, our boys after taking a region title; my mother because who loves you more? – the Chattahoochee River – my dad - seven smiling girls after winning our first cross country title in our 28 year history of the sport. There's another one – I won't mention her name but her initials are Jackie Addy – and she's crossing the finish line in route to her individual championship.

The Sheryl picture was "The Art of Walking Through Greenville on Christmas." Problem was, nothing was open. Still, the night rocked anyway. As for Jackie, it evokes the memory of Jayaraj commenting that she would take off after a jet plane at the starting line if she had the chance. I laugh, because I remember telling him that she was young and talented, and Las Vegas odds said she'd probably catch it.

And as for the seven girls: They are small and dainty like most cross country kids are. You can usually fit two or three of them in the car of your console, with their angles and elbows and knobby knees, braces on some of the faces, medals around their necks.

There's another of my dad, who was a miler at New Hampshire. He was an artist and a pharmacist and he built houses and caught fish and did taxidermy and was close to being a genius. Though I captured his love for the written word, unfortunately I only got half his IQ.

Still, I'll take it. And this picture of him while he's concentrating on his drawing, the same expression of a runner about to make his or her kick, the same finish line taunting and daunting, yet egging him on. That look alone is an attractor factor on some days.

It's a slideshow now. Sheryl. Mom. Dad. The river. Jackie. That group of seven whose names I'll never forget, and they are Reese and Hayden and another Reese and Emily and Maddie, and Erin, and Jessica. Some of them have flown away, their feathers too bright to stay in one place or even in our sport.

I refrained from crying at their graduation but it didn't keep me from hugging their necks – pandemic and six feet apart be darned. My connection with them – and all these pictures – are our connection with my soul and my selfish desire for happiness.

In closing, when God took me off the factory, he gave me very little ambition. I want to be the president of absolutely nothing, have zero desire to tell anyone what to do or when or how to do it. Live gently, I say, and leave something behind. As dad used to say, "Leave 'em laughing."

I'll just settle for leaving them smiling. And when I'm having trouble doing that, I simply stare at a screen in Groesbeck Hall, Room 410, and I do so for only one reason: It makes me happy.

Period.

CHALK TALK

The senior took the piece of chalk and walked forward – the fact that he's a senior defies time, gravity, and all rational sense. Before I blinked, he was a wide-eyed freshman, a deer in headlights, someone we had to coax not to the finish line, but to the start.

And you, one of the coaches, are sitting in the background while this guy, this boy – no, this man, this senior – is looking at the state course map and he's going over it line by line, sharing his experience and reading the minds of the younger even before the starting gun goes off.

"You'll go out too hard right HERE, and that will be dumb. Remember, it's a 3-mile race. At this point, you need to start picking people off, one by one by one. It's kind of hypnotic, it is, and you the writer are sitting out there thinking, "Wow, I wish I could write stuff like this."

It's cross country chalk talk – you thought it was reserved for football but humans know how to make lines, graphs and coordinates out of everything. Nothing simple is spared, no slam dunk taken for granted. Often this bugs you, but as for now you're eating it up.

Because you watched this senior three years ago have little experience and even less confidence, and you have a priceless unwritten job description in that you get to see this man become the man with the chalk, this man making sense of coordinates and graphs and things that instantly recall D-minus grades on your own papers.

Your eyes go to these wide-eyed freshmen, ones you pray will have the strength to take the hills on the second loop at state in Carrollton tomorrow, then at the same time applaud them for being there, for being forced to sprout wings even before they were cleared for takeoff.

A scouting report came out in August and they weren't even on it – had to look up their names in the Family Directory where you could spell them correctly on the roster. They walked up nervously that first day at the river, all stutters and heads down and never looking you in the eye.

You smiled then, because you didn't see a freshman but a nervous human on the launching pad though they didn't and don't have the years to see it that way yet. Still, you know – beyond all knowing – they are scared on the outside but you're locking them in soul to soul – and you can't believe you get paid to watch them take off before your very eyes.

The hard part, you see, is when they go, and dealing with the pain when they're going, going, gone. You will conjure up memories trying to bring them back, but as the great philosopher once said, "Life can only be understood backwards, but it must be lived forwards."

So, you watch the man with the chalk speak to the ones on the pad – you marvel at the resiliency of this youth that lives in a world where nothing – and you mean nothing – is penned in on any schedule. Cancellations are the norm, detours are expected, and yet they're still here and they're listening to the man with the chalk and they are so young but they're not. They're really not.

They are already, in fact, so much older than you're ready for. You fight wars in your head because you want them to grow, but then again, you don't. You're trapped in your head about when and how to step in and the more painful moment of stepping the hell out of the way.

It's the getting out of the way part that hurts the most,

you say – and you say this as a man who has never been a parent.

Still, the man with the chalk is finished. He puts it on the board. The younger kids clap. It's state they are preparing for, but there are so much more pure things at stake than how they will finish, or if they will stand on a rung of a podium that may or may not even be presented.

They are still here despite everything that is thrown at them. And you can't figure out where your heart flies out the most – to the man with the chalk or the younger ones listening.

God look after them all…

ON THE EIGHTH DAY...

On the eighth day, God invented track and field - and while he was on a roll – he put in the 11th commandment to boot. "Thou shalt make the 4 X 400-meter relay the last event of the day."

I had to laugh the other night while watching our girls pass that sacred baton back and forth. Oh the times I've seen that stick dropped onto the track, and those hearts that dropped with it. Our boys lost state two years in a row in that race, the total distance was about the space between these two words.

Still, you have to love watching kids and grownups alike, filming with their phones, jumping up and down, kids trampling over each other at the finish line to get a good look. No, I don't really know who invented all this, though I do know it was James Naismith who came up with basketball, and I couldn't care less who spawned mixed martial arts.

Regardless, it wasn't only about our girls winning the region title and the excitement of the 4 X 400 - it was about consistency.

Our 800-meter boy - let's call him Aidan since that's his name - ran the fastest 800 in his life - broke two minutes in the process. I went to congratulate him but was trampled by his teammates who were waiting to get at him. The shoe marks on my back were all worth it. Besides, I need to do laundry anyway.

It was a good site watching young Aidan - a shy lad if there ever was one - getting mobbed by his peers. I love the fact that you don't have to be outgoing to be popular.

It's like water hitting a rock - you just keep showing up and you just keep showing up and one day you're breaking records and your teammates are mobbing you for it.

That's the way it works. As it should. And thank God.

Anyway, my thoughts are at the start/finish of that relay - and it was a neat sight watching one girl pass the baton to the next with only one word to offer: "RUN!" She did, for the record, and you simply couldn't help getting caught up in it, even though I don't even know who the heck she is or was nor what team she was running for.

It helped that our girls stood on the top of the podium when the night was over, though I can assure you we've had races where we were almost forced to walk under it. They were so excited they forgot their bags and their books and their yoga mats and their drinks.

Not their phones, though. Let's not get carried away.

Anyway, bless you all who put in the time to coach track, and my love to all who show up in the dead of winter to take part in any form or fashion. It's simplistic - you run and jump and play and throw things. We've made it complicated - because that's what we humans do.

Still, it's simple. Not much fancy equipment required. Singlet. Shoes. Maybe a watch. Throw in some water or some Power Ade.

Sorry for rambling; these are just thoughts left over from the sleep I didn't get last night. A baton dropped in my head and I woke up screaming at 3:30 in the morning. It'll be okay, though. Summer's approaching - baseball games, concerts, catching up on sleep, chilling out with friends or a good book, travel.

It's not the 4 X 400 relay or anything, but it'll have to do.

THE MINDSET OF THE POLE VAULTER

Three years ago, I stood on the track with one of my runners, and I'll never forget what she said. "Track is so random! You throw things, jump into sand, jump over bars, pass batons, run fast, run slow, and then there's that pole vault thing."

Yes, there is "that pole vault thing", where the "need for speed" meets "height feels right." Just where and what is the attraction of an event that requires the speed of the runway, the precision of the steps in inserting the pole, the strength of lift-off, the grace of getting over the bar, and the happy landing…or at least one can hope?

"In a way, it's simply the art of being psychotic," one vaulter said with a laugh. "Still, there's a good feeling doing an event that a lot of people can't do. I mean, you can't just hop into the pole vault. It's also rather primal – you're elevated 14 feet in the air by a stick and you give up control."

Is giving up control a good thing? Is it the adrenaline of it all? Not to date myself, but in the late 70s, high school pole vault was the easy way to qualify for state and miss school an extra day. The negative was, the "landing pits" were often surrounded by plywood, and I witnessed more than twice our vaulter landing on wood or asphalt, instead of cushion.

Still, he – like so many others before and after him – continue to grab the pole, that pole that's hard to even get TO the meets, that pole that requires moving your spare tire and back seat around just to fit it in there.

"I like watching people do the event, and I think it's a rush to be 13 feet in the air, upside down, backwards, whatever. It's just fun." This is from a vaulter who – in an off season accident, shattered his hand and wasn't supposed to be able to grab a toothbrush, much less a pole. He ended as a two-year state champion.

In moving on, it's not just the vaulters that get in on the "height is right" thing, as a former Florida coach Roy Benson added: "I once had to verify a world record set at 18, feet, 6 ½ inches at the Florida Relays. It was scary climbing up unwieldly stepladders to verify new records. It's not just the vaulters who get to see the world from a scary perspective."

Ex-high school coach Bill Railey phrased it this way: "It's a tough event to watch, it's a tough event to participate in, and it's a tough event to coach. But when it's done right, it's unbelievable!"

Whether a rush or psychotic, adrenaline-filled or all in between, the former "easy way to get to state" is now an event that proves to be a marathon without the miles at track meets – and yes, even at the high school level.

Okay, so now we have an event that requires speed, strength, and precision – to name only some, plus it's something that takes up a lot of time. So in a world where many dream of scoring the winning touchdown, hitting the walk-off homer, or scoring the game-winning goal, where does pole vault fit into all this?

Perhaps the answer can be summed up the way a former high school state-qualifying vaulter did, when asked what drew her in.

"I'm not really sure…"

Another put it this way: "It's like a violent ballet of sorts…"

It is what it is – an event that requires multiple skill sets, not to mention timing and balance. So – in closing and to all you pole vaulters out there, regardless of whatever the attractions may or may not be: May your elevations always increase and your bellies or back sides never move that ever-raised bar.

Oh, and one other thing: May your landings always be safe, soft, and sound…

THE LITTLE THINGS

I'm standing on the track infield – just watching. I do this often, it's the writer in me. Our girls are in one stretching circle, the boys about eight yards away in another. It's Friday, they are laughing, happy, a bunch of active verbs temporarily halted by a comma before their weekend.

It seems two of them are going hiking; one can't get off this spirit animal thing; another seems to think it's a great idea to run his cool down with fins on. Another is sprinting – literally – between soccer and track.

This running thing has made them close, earned them friends. If you want to get competitive about it, their times are dropping, there is improvement out here in every pair of feet.

For some reason, a Brene Brown quotes pops into my head, one I'll have to paraphrase since I don't feel like looking it up. "Life is composed of little things; we often miss it because we're looking for the big ones."

Yeah that, or something close.

The little things – one of them being there's not much editing with the high school kid. It's fresh, random, often way out from left field. Once, while subbing, one of my kids superglued a dead fly to a post-It note. Another day, one approached the desk and asked if she could "go on an adventure." Seriously, not only where does this come from, but how exactly do you respond to it?

You think you've heard it all, but you haven't. You really haven't. The trick is not to analyze, but to enjoy it, let it amuse you as it should. Write it down if you must.

The little things – a simple walk down our halls for

example. Many days, it's very similar to being in an Improv class. They will tell you something, you must quickly off the top of your head respond, keep the conversation going. If your reply dams up the momentum, you've failed.

In thinking about it, this isn't such a little thing after all. It keeps you young. This reminds me of another thing I read – somewhere – about "not letting an old guy in." I think that was Clint Eastwood, who's still producing movies as an 80-year-old.

Or another one, "How old would you be if you didn't know when you were born?" That was either Satchel Paige or a country and western song – the fact you can never remember is why you never made good on term papers in high school in the first place.

After all, you're supposed to cite the book, the page, the paragraph. For some reason, throwing up your arms and saying, "Heck, I don't remember," never was a good enough for most English teachers.

Or all of them for that matter.

But back to the track. Two are putting on their spikes, ready to sprint. The hurdlers are finished, you're not sure if they ran faster on the track or now, when leaving for their Friday night. The pole vaulters are putting the tarp back on, collecting those long, awkward sticks that are so adventurous to haul around. Who invented that anyway?

One of your distance runners, I think but I'm not sure, is asleep in Lane 6.

I get it, I'm supposed to awaken him, perhaps motivate him with one of my 'speeches." Still, laughing is legal, too, right? This may be the most sleep the kid gets all weekend, right there, natural style, with spring sunlight tanning his almost zit-free face.

The little things – and the gratitude for it all. If you'd have told me at the age of 60, I was going to be coaching track at a high school, and subbing on top of that, I would've cried on the spot – ran to the nearest watering hole and drank my "troubles" away.

In moving on, it's also knowing what to throw out, since there are these sayings that people deliver that you're just supposed to not only believe but live by. For example, "A million people can't be wrong." Sure they can. Ten million people bought the album "Saturday Night Fever." Seventy thousand paid to see Wrestlemania in the Pontiac Silverdome. Nixon was elected in a landslide. Mixed martials arts is bringing in millions if not billions.

Find your own rhythm, I say, like these kids are doing right here, right now. Jackson Browne nailed it in one of his songs, "For a Dancer." I think it's on his "Late for the Sky," LP, but I could be wrong about that. Take that English teachers, I'm pretty sure I got that one.

Oh well, enough of my mental wanderings. I must be off myself. After all, my verbs are all finished, even my Lane 6 'hotel guest' is up and stirring, wiping the drool off his face as he's doing so. They are headed into their nights which, at this age, will more than probably blend into tomorrow.

I get a little sad when thinking of this. My tonight will probably end before The Goldbergs are over at 9:00, the time I used to be headed into the unknown. Regardless, there are lots of walls I'd like to be flies on; there's so many stories out there but not enough ink in my pen to keep up with them all.

For now, though, I'm grateful they are all here, just as one day I'll have to be grateful to let them all go. As I've written, this can be hard – really hard. And maybe I do know a little bit of what it's like to be a parent after all.

Still, I laugh. They are getting better. They are bonding. If they never change, it's okay with me. I hear them laughing.

I turn back for one last look…and they are gone…

THE ENIGMA OF THE 4 X 100-METER RELAY

Years ago, I read a book titled, "The Boys in the Boat" and it was about rowing. To be clear, you could put what I know about that sport in a thimble and still have room to spare, but I was fascinated by the symmetry, the cohesiveness, the teamwork, and the flow that MUST happen in order for the team to succeed.

Eight can be great, but if one body movement is off, if one zigs instead of zags, if one lifts instead of drops, sacred time is lost, the gold medal floats away while you drift in behind another boat's wake.

Along with this, I had a conversation with our head track coach about the 4 X 100-meter relay the other day, and how our men's Olympic team can't seem to hold on to this little stick thingie known as the baton. Americans run fast, do they not? There's plenty of training and facilities around, right?

Not to take anything away from the 4 X 400 or the 4 X 800, but you can drop the precious stick at the high school level, pick it up, and have a chance. If there's the merest bobble in the 4 X 100, game over.

"There are so many ways you can mess it up," our coach said. "You drop the baton, you're done. You can go out of your lane, you can go out of the exchange zone, or you can just simply get beat."

This fascinates my simplistic brain, as I grew up with the painful art of being a 2-miler. The 3,200, in all due respect, is pretty cut and dry. You run eight laps, and you hopefully do it fast enough to make the audience dizzy as opposed to putting them to sleep. It's will and guts that often get you through it, and in all due respect to the "no I in team," at this point you have to know that there is an "M" and an "E", as there's not a whole lot any of them can do when there's two laps left and your legs have turned to spaghetti.

But the 4 X 100? It's a work of art, so beautiful you could put music to it when it works. It's fast and furious – the fastest of the fastest combining into one four-person symphony – think the Beatles if you will but with the results taking a lot less than three minutes.

I listen in at practice, at the art of putting them in the right order. To the casual eye, what does it matter? They're all fast. Just take that stick and haul butt. Try it sometime. Like most pieces of art, there's contemplation involved, the movement of pieces around, shuffling this way and that. She's fast but can she give it and pass it? Who comes off the starting blocks best? Why can't he seem to give it to him? Who invented this sport, anyway?"

In closing, I'll always be a distance man. Still, the adrenaline of the 4 X 100 will always fascinate me, how four – no matter how fast – must become one.

And like "The Boys in the Boat," it is indeed a puzzle. But once you see the finished product, it's a blaze of speed that can only inspire, even if the four aren't on your team.

AN IMAGINARY GUN LAP – A TALE OF WOE FROM 2020

Today's track meet -- like everything else -- has been cancelled.

I think for sanity's sake I'll walk down to our track, yellow note pad in hand, and watch imaginary coaches start their watches, hear them tell their kids to "work this lap," and "two to go, get up there," and "you've got this."

Will see the starter tell and warn the kids around the finish line to stand back where the timers can see. The kids will listen -- for at least six seconds -- before the adrenaline of the finish kicks in and all are screaming. I'll actually smile inside while I envision that scene -- that safe chaos where all hell breaks loose at another photo finish.

Maybe I'll go back in time, through the years, and feel one of my former senior's adrenaline when he's on the fourth lap trying to break the sacred 5-minute mile, will scream out of habit at my top girl not to run the first lap too fast, will shoot healthy vibes into one of my wounded girls' legs -- praying those shin splints don't rear their ugly head(s).

In perspective, it's the smallest of the small, though sanity matters no matter who you are. It's sort of ironic -- they tell you the smartest thing you can do is go home and stay there -- don't contaminate the world.

I live alone -- I'm a self-contained human being for the most part. And I don't usually need to go where everybody knows my name.

Still, sometimes it's good to be in a place where at least somebody does…

THE RHYTHM OF THE MORNING RUN

It's 5:30 a.m. - do you know where your running shoes are? There they are, lined up against the wall, each pair ready for you to call their name. It's early, you couldn't care less – all you know is your mind is a cesspool times twelve and on steroids and you simply HAVE to move.

It's something you read – if your mind's not working, work on the body. If the body's not working, work on the mind. It's the rabid squirrels of the mind that's the problem as you tear off the sheets, the lack of sleep due to a soccer story typo and Mother's Day approaching and track season finishing and a dentist appointment looming and the stress of carpool.

You grab two shoes, hoping to God they match, or at least there's a left one and a right. On this day, you get it right, so on they go and off you go, as there's a track at work near your office. It's obviously dark out due to the hour once you get there, and you can hear your footsteps slicing through the grass. The starting line is over there – right there – and you have a sense of dread as you approach.

Martin Luther King had it right, you know. "You don't have to see the whole staircase, just take the first step." Ah, that first step, the beginning, the hardest thing ever whether it's running, writing, making the sales call or life in general. Breaking through the inertia. Movement after stillness. It's all momentum when you think about it – the idea is to get it going on YOUR side – physically and mentally.

Out of habit and years of training, you start, you move, and the first step as a 60-year-old is a tough one –

picture a mannequin that the establishment forgot to oil. It's a roll call of body parts, each one creaking for attention, though eventually they relent – allow – let the show go on.

It takes a lap or maybe two, but eventually the rhythm kicks in, albeit a slow one. The sweat starts to smooth the mattress marks on your face, the thoughts start to line themselves up – like water before going down a drain.

There are other lunatics like me out here – some Atlanta Track Club people meet up twice a week and you can hear their chatter and times and the like as they pass you ever so easily. Once a sore spot, now you smile at this, and it makes you remember why you run with a GPS instead of an App.

An App, after all, shouts out your pace. At least the GPS has the good sense to shut the hell up, lets you run in peace. And in rhythm.

Your body and mind are teaming up now as you near the end. The sun – almost on cue – starts to peak over Mt. Vernon and lights are coming on in our sacred hallways. You smile, not just because you're moving but because the chaotic order that is a high school hallway. Lockers slamming. Kids flirting. Book bags hoisted over those small shoulders.

You cross not the finish line, but a finish line – and as you turn off your watch you hope there's many more to follow assuming the years, the bones, and the muscles allow.

Still, you can't help but grin, as there's a full day ahead – carpool and class and carpool again and practice and paperwork and scores to collect. It's okay though.

After all, you have started – and you are three miles better of a person because of it.

THE ART OF COACHING TRACK

There was a time in my life when the last thing I wanted to do was coach track.

The meets were and are WAY too long, was my first thought. Seriously, the sun comes up, it peaks high, it goes down again and you're still out there, charting races and paces and looking for kids and wondering who's going to run the last leg of the 4-by-4.

On some days, you get frostbite in the morning, followed by sunburn in the afternoon, back to frostbite. And again, you're still out there.

I'm reminded of an incident three years ago – though this is cross country related - when one of our football coaches drew the short straw and had to drive the spirit bus to the state championships in Carrollton in November. I think for him, like a lot of people, cross country meets meant running in towns that aren't on maps, and across courses that take you past cows and hay bales and remote fields that one can only hope has been plowed in the last week or so.

In a way, a lot of these people would, in a lot of ways, be right.

Then – in both of the above cases - a starting gun was fired. And the noise level went from a 1 to a 9 on the decibel scale. And grand dads and grand moms lifted out of those chairs they had before been glued to. Suddenly friendly spectators got rude in boxing out for space at finish lines. Cameras were aimed, locked, loaded and fired.

In short, adrenaline happened with a double ought exclamation point. This, after all, is a Law of Attraction type Universe, where energy begets energy – it circles through the course and back again. To quote from our football coach after the fact, "That was AWESOME!"

I write this on a day where we do indeed have a track meet. It's 30 degrees out, but it's going up to 65. How exactly do you dress for these things – this sport that takes hours on end? After all, most games are easy – they last two hours or so and the weather is what the weather is.

Track people face all four seasons in one day – the winds of March meet the frost of January, the bloomy trees make you think it's spring or fall, and after a lap or two, you catch a hint of summer.

Again, what to wear?

And the answer is a beautiful thing, because you have to prepare for it all. Not just in the climate, but in loading up the poles, and piecing together your relay teams. Texting your throwers who will often be in remote and hidden places while they – often unseen – do their things. Spike and lace up the shoes for the sprinters, relay the splits of the distance runners, go over the tactics for the jumpers and the hurdlers.

It's such a random thing, this track sport I help coach, but that in itself forces you to open up your brain a bit. It's not a zoned-in history class, though I can assure you, the education is just as valuable, the lessons learned, the tears and triumphs of staring at that watch at race's end will teach a kid so much about handling success. And failure. And life.

Anyway – as I said – there was a time when I didn't want to coach track. It takes too long. I freeze and burn and freeze again. And there I still am.

But then one day, like so many others before me, a gun went off.

And a whole world of education followed closely thereafter…

RUNNING: SO MANY WAYS TO WIN

Three years ago: I'm standing at the finish line at the Asics Invitational, waiting on my last JV runner to come through. He runs at dump truck pace on a good day, but with the laser heat and the muddy course from last night's rain, he's started this race slow and he appears to be tapering.

All of a sudden, a runner from another school taps me on the shoulder. "What's his name?" he asks. He's pointing to my kid, who has about 500 meters to go before he's finished. Confused at first, I'm not sure how to react. Does this guy want to make fun of him? Why does he want to know his name? Do I tell him?

For some reason, I did, and off the athlete went – across the finish chute, into the woods, and he joined my runner down the home stretch. Curious now, I follow their progress as they head onto the final straightaway. The opposing runner is not only pacing my athlete but is exciting the crowd and getting them to shout out my athlete's name

"Ken! Ken! Ken!"

Slowly but surely, the chant catches on. My athlete, with sweat, spit, dirt, and mud coming out every pore, smiles big – all 32 teeth on deck – as he crosses the line. My kid doesn't stop his watch; he never started one – but he's in it to finish it. And he did.

This story makes me smile. Because this sport isn't just for the people who break the tape, climb to the highest rung on the podium, always go home with bling wrapped around their neck followed by their names in the paper. At best, some may or may not get a certificate at the year-end banquet, will pose for the obligatory team picture, then move on to their winter sport.

Back to present day, one of my JV kids approached me just last week and had this to say, "I just want to get where I can break the 6-minute mile." He might. He might not. Either way, he wins, as he's setting his mind, getting focused, zeroing in.

And another point, my runner who breaks 4:30 won't look down his nose at him but will be one of the first to congratulate him at the finish regardless. I've seen my share of post-race celebrations, and I can honestly say I've seen just as many or more for the people who did NOT finish first.

A great bond it is, that perseverance, and that pain, and crossing that finish line. You either get it or you don't, and no lack of respect for those who don't. Still, I can't help but to laugh when talking to those who don't.

"You're going to run how many miles? On Saturday? They tilt their head when they ask this; back up a step whereas not to catch whatever it is you have. Their tone suggests that you have seven eyeballs on your face, or an extra giant zit on your forehead.

I'm all for competition, have perhaps never smiled so bright in November of 2019 in Carrollton when our girls broke a glass ceiling and climbed to the top rung of a podium. But here's to my boy Ken, that energetic opponent who got him some love, and all who are toeing the line for whatever thousands of reasons you're toeing it for.

And here's to the tortoise and the hares and all in between. It's great to be out there again, where – the way I see it – as long as you keep moving forward, there really aren't that many ways you can lose.

COLD WEATHER TRACK COACHING

It's mid-February – track practice time – and where in the world are they? There they come, clad in short pants and a t-shirt even though it's 36 degrees outside with the wind chill set at a balmy 25. One of your girls actually has on a tank top; you're prone to exaggerate as a writer but you can almost swear you see icicles coming off both her shoulder blades.

You're clad in 17 layers; you had on a hat but the 30 mile-per-hour winds just blew it somewhere between Roswell Road and Hammond. You had feet when you left your office, but the feeling of those 10 toes left somewhere between the starting line and the 100-meter mark.

Still, life goes on and those kids -- who will live forever and cold weather doesn't even exist -- simply flirt and giggle and set their watches while they wait. You give them the workout, but who can understand a word with your mask on? At the risk of spreading germs to your kids and the unsuspecting public, you lower it and speak clearly, or at least you think you do.

Off they go for their mile warm-up. One of your girls, that poor thing, only weighs about 74 pounds so the wind moves her from lanes 1 to 4 to 6 and back again. Still, there's a good story going on among the four of them so none of them seem to notice. They just bob and sway and giggle and jog. You laugh, or you try to, though your words get coughed out, muffled; they succeed then immediate fail at making any sense -- think an AM radio on static if you will.

Suddenly, your trainer appears on the steps. He's a sane soul, dressed in four coats, a hat, and gloves, and his voice is VERY clear as he yells across the lanes. "Put on your warm-ups and your sweats! This is a rule. You can NOT be out here in shorts and a t-shirt." The kids stop, look up, ponder. One puts her hand on her side, kicks her foot out, considers, and then, "Do we have to?"

As for you, you wonder. What makes a real feel 25-degree day NOT be cold to high school kids? Do you have to reach a certain age? Does your skin thin with the election of each new president, or on odd leap years?

Still, you're wise, or at least you should be. You calculate the effort of the one-mile split, into a monsoon, using only Coach Jayaraj's brain and your #2 pencil. He figures two of those, then a 20-minute cooldown, with the wind, then stretch. Indoors.

Your kids roll their eyes, laugh at how old you are, wonder just what the problem is. In their world, they are outside, not in a class, no one is lecturing, so why can't they just run and jump and play?

Off they go, or shall you say, off they blow - around that track. You yourself have rocks in your pocket, ballast if you will, though the youth just choose to battle the elements they don't even feel and are yet to understand. Still, you've learned – go with the flow – whatever that happens to be at the moment.

With that, you watch them stick and move, dodge and weave, as they giggle off into the sunset. As for you, you throw your clipboard into the air, and you laugh while it blows into the wild blue yonder - probably to join that hat you once owned.

MEDITATIONS FROM THE STARTING LINE

Did you train enough? Did you train too much? Where's the bathroom? Are your shoes laced up? Why is this obnoxious guy trying to talk to you at the starting line? What pace are you going out at? Where's the first hill? How did you get into this crazy sport anyway?

These questions pound your head as you stand there, and you stand there doing the worst possible thing – you're waiting. It's six minutes until gun time, six whole minutes, and you just had to take your warmups off and you're cold and it's windy and you didn't sleep worth a damn, and you may be catching a cold that could lead to pneumonia that could…

Breathe. Best advice ever. You simply breathe – deep. You remember the advice of your mother – she used to make you breathe and count to ten. Nothing else. Let it go, like the passing of the clouds. That's what thoughts should be anyway, right – just passing clouds…

The problem is you're holding on to each one – you're not enjoying the parade because you keep following one of the floats along. You shake out your shoulders, your arms, your neck, you recheck your shoes for the ninth time.

Mr. Chatterbox won't leave you alone. He's going on about his shoes – who gives a rat's damn about anybody's shoes? Seriously! And something about his last race – for some reason it's important that you know his splits at his last 14 races. And there you stand, not really sure what you should go in at this one.

Three minutes until gun time. You have to pee. You always have to pee. What's the answer here – coffee before a race? Sure, great idea, but there's always a line at the bathrooms and they always smell worse than a sewer. And there's always that one person – that one – who takes FOREVER to get out.

You hate bathroom chatter anyway. You ever want to hear a horrible joke? Go pee. Anywhere! "If you shake it more than once you're playing with it." How many times have you heard that? Is that supposed to be funny?

The thought of it ticks you off, while here you stand, supposedly getting ready to race.

Two minutes. You wish you'd learned to meditate, train your mind, go into the gap. Gap? What gap? There's 1000 words per minute flying around in here, where in the hell is this gap people keep talking about.

You catch a break. Mr. Talkative finds someone else to bother, though it bothers you that people can't read your body language when they're bothering you. Can't people get it? Did you look like you care what size shoe he has on?

One minute. You've forgotten to keep your legs moving. Great idea, you tell yourself. You warm up for 20 minutes, only to stand here the last six and let your legs go dead again. Good thinking…

Finally, a voice appears, a man with a bullhorn, his early morning syllables slicing through the tense air. He talks…for too long…even though he probably only spoke for a few seconds or so.

You look at your watch. The gun's supposed to be fired. Let's go. Shut up already. Shoot. The. Gun!

"Runner's set!"

Longest second in eternity, between 'runner's set' and that sacred gun. Shoot it for crying out loud. Shoot it! Shoot it!

Finally, the gun fires, releasing you from your mental misery.

Now it's time to tackle the physical one…

NINETEEN MINUTES, FIFTY-TWO SECONDS

0:00: - She seems so calm, which I find a bit odd. Usually on race day – or Vision Quest Day as I have often referred to it - you are antsy times twelve mentally and physically.

We're on I-20 if that matters – it's early; cross country early as we like to say. It's the dynamic of the sport. Football players go off to hell in the summer for camp. Baseball players spend spring break somewhere in Florida. Basketball troops spend Thanksgiving and Christmas holidays traveling to tournaments. Well? Cross country runners get up at dark-thirty on Saturday mornings and run in exotic fields across the state.

It's what we do.

Now let me back up even further. 'She' is Bryn – a sophomore - and her quest is to break the twenty-minute barrier in the 5K. She's been close, close enough to continue to pour gas on the fire of her dream. And she's been frustrated because she hasn't made it yet.

We've texted about these near misses. "You're almost there!" "Don't quit!" I even tried my hand at being a Star Wars, Yoda-like character when I texted her: "Trust the journey!" These are some of my texts, but like emails, they usually get deleted in my normal 'clear your clutter, clear your mind' manner.

I check my mirror and most are either asleep or tuned into their music. This always fascinates me – these pre-race rituals. I love to see how the kids get motivated. Some rock out, pace, punch things. Others sit silently, gaze off into forever. Some joke and gather around. Others go into solitude. And as I said, some of them simply sleep…

It's these differences and habits of the teenage mind that keeps me loving what I do. The kids of today - they're not bad, they're just a bunch of hyperactive verbs. You want a conversation with a kid in the hall? Don't expect them to stop – they've got places to go. You either speak quickly or you walk with them. The old-fashioned sort might consider this rude – maybe think they should stop when an adult speaks. Nope, welcome to the 21st century, where verbs will continue to be verbs, no commas required.

"How'd you sleep last night, Bryn?" I ask before she goes off into Margaritaville with Buffett or Friends in Low Places with Garth. She smiles – she's all teeth when she does this – all 32 of them come front and center.

My mind cranks into hyper mode when she answers, "I slept like a rock!" This too is highly unusual the night before game day. A good night's sleep before a big game is usually an oxymoron. Thoughts gather, wait in line while scenarios are played out – good and bad. Each thought waits to enter, ready to dive in like kids into a pool on the first day of summer.

Still, that's her answer. She smiles again when she says it; props her feet up, plugs in the ear phones, goes off into Teenage-Space Land. Me, I drive. Forty-two miles to go and ninety-two minutes to do it in. As of this very moment, life is good.

* * *

We pull in somewhere in the middle of a field – wait in line while the parking attendant points to plot T somewhere between the biggest, longest buses ever. Great chance of getting blocked in but I'm not worried about that now.

As the kids gather their belongings and get off, my

eyes are taking this all in, as the youth grab pillows and blankets and phones, book bags, athletic bags, spikes and even teddy bears. Some still have mattress marks on their little faces. Many seem a little ticked off about this 'early morning Saturday thing.' The veterans are used to it – they'll be laughing with each other before we even get the tent put up. Eventually the sleepers will follow suit.

All will get comfortable eventually, some even resting against the other. The serious ones will be nervous. The not so serious perhaps wondering how they got into all this. Regardless, it's the calm before the storm and each, at some point, will have to think about what they're here for.

It's what happens.

Coach Jayaraj has them warm up approximately fifty minutes before show time. It's the beauty of preparation – the kids know what to do. They will run for around ten minutes, do their dynamic stretch, and then make their last minute adjustments to their spikes or their hair or their clothes.

Bryn will have to pin her jersey on tighter – it's two sizes too big. I'm not sure if we ran out of the new uniforms or if she was too slow to get in the line. Either way, the uniforms are new and pretty and they stand out, but just like the old ones, hers is too big.

Still, the rituals and the nerves are all over the place now. I can feel it as I circle the tent. "Do you have an extra pin?" "Remember to tie your chip in tight!" "Tape up your shoes if you have to. Do we have any more tape?"

Words are starting to spill out at five hundred words per minute with gusts up to seven-fifty. Little bodies are scurrying, hurrying. Hell, I'm even getting a little nervous myself.

At twelve minutes before, they begin the walk to the starting line. It's about hundred-plus meters away. They must do their strides, meet at the end of their first one, huddle together in each other's' arms – talk about things. Like the smile thing, the huddle is something that makes me just stand and watch. In fact, I often don't even wonder what they're saying; I feel it's something they and they alone deserve.

No coaches, no parents, no lectures – let them work it out. What they say is none of my business – and I'm one of the coaches.

Eventually they un-arm themselves and sprint back. Then forth. Back. Forth.

Bryn and our team captain – Izzy - are talking. Izzy is a senior veteran; she usually gets quiet and doesn't like to be bothered. The two train together, though, so they have roots. In fact, last year they even joked about being each other's conscience. It's funny, but when you really are into running that actually makes sense in a funny, demented kind of way.

Regardless, both heads come together at the front of the line, running plans mapped, planned, coordinated. They hug. They are ready. The team bunches in together, adjusts their watches, wait impatiently while some race director goes through his spiel.

They've heard it before – most have anyway. At this late season point, they only want to hear one thing. Eventually, they do.

A starting gun goes off in Douglasville.

6:15: Bryn goes through the mile right on schedule, but there is a problem – a big problem. It rained last night – pretty hard – so she's already sloshed through a couple of puddles; almost slipped a time or two.

Her start was fast, but not (state champ) Serena

Tripodi fast as she was instructed. It's sort of the oxymoron of a race: you're told not to go out too fast, but if you don't get out pretty fast you get lost in the shuffle; boxed in with the field.

It's tricky, but you need to go out reasonably fast and then settle in fast, if that makes any sense. Lots of running things are tricky. For example, she was told all summer that she needed to train slower where she could race faster. If you're not a runner, that may make no sense. If you are, you get it.

In looking back, my summer runs with her were social but with that very point: You have to run at 'Dunn' pace. Her eyes would roll but she would smile again, adjust her watch and off we would go. Just as often, there wasn't much conversation except for me telling her to slow down, to stay with me. She would laugh. "Oh, I forgot! We're running at Dunn pace!"

If we turned her loose, every jog would be a race. Her mind can do it but last year her shins could not. She was in a stress fracture boot by November. Again, it happens.

Our laughs would give way to our feet pounding away at the trail of the river. It was hot out, more reason to keep it slow. When you're older you get that too, though perhaps too late. Verbs, however, don't understand it yet.

Summer is only a memory for now though. The pools are all closed. It's October, decades have happened in a kid's life. And none of it matters. Except this. Now. It's time for the second mile.

13:04: It's muddy and the sun has come out – neither conducive for achieving a Vision Quest. Still, her legs chug forward, Coach Jayaraj's voice still in her head.

Jayaraj is a passionate man and Bryn a driven athlete. The two work together in a cohesive way, though she - having the typical Type-A mentality of the distance runner - sometimes wonders if she's working hard enough. "The clock won't lie," Jayaraj always says. "I'd rather you run faster on Saturdays than on Tuesdays."

She will acknowledge, accept, and as she said to me after my Yoda text, eventually admit: "I believe you."

On she runs. She's tired and her heart is in it, but – as Jayaraj's voice fills her mind – the clock won't wait.

19:47: Three miles are down, but now for the dreaded point-one. That's one hundred, eighty-five yards for those of you scoring at home, and it can be the toughest thing there is.

She rounds the corner and sees the finish, looks at her watch, hears the crowd. She's sixth overall – more than great for a sophomore racing against bigger schools. Still – like the normal mindset of an achieving kid – this isn't enough. The clock is ticking…ticking… She doesn't think she'll make it.

Her heart sinks but her legs do not. She runs like she's trained to run. Those miles, those summer trails, those early morning jogs around the neighborhood, they're never for nothing.

Champions don't quit. They don't fail either, not for long. The clock passes 20:00 but she shrugs it off. She sprints for all she's worth and crosses the finish line. The clock reads 20:34. Briefly, she is sad, frustrated, wanting to scream.

She looks down. She has 19:52 written on her hand; it's been written there daily for the last two months. Did she do something wrong? Did she train too hard? Not hard enough? Why didn't she make it?

She hears a voice. It's Izzy who came in right behind her. And there comes Kate, and Megan, and Molly, all the way down the line.

FINISH: They huddle again. She is hugged by all teammates. They all know her, love her, respect her. She hasn't failed at anything. The captain and the rock – tells her how good she did. Tells her she has nothing to be ashamed of and she "ran awesome!" Izzy did well herself – as did the rest of the sweaty, muddy clan.

Deep down she knows it, accepts it, believes it. She has come to trust, love and respect Izzie and her teammates the way she does the sport. Runners, like the clock, don't lie. You either put it all out there or you don't. She and the captain always do. All the younger teammates are starting to get it also.

It's simply one of the great things about sports that are hard to explain. Still, if you work hard, it's what happens.

I walk away from the huddle out of respect. It's their moment. Still, I look. Bryn is smiling now. They all are.. And right about…now…I hear a camera go off.

Someone has photographed this moment in time – a time when ten cross country girls just put it on the line for perhaps ten different reasons. Some wanted to break twenty, some wanted to win the team trophy, some just wanted to finish to go off and enjoy their long weekends.

Still, they all did it. And on their faces shows achievement, sacrifice, guts, a "we did it" look on the faces of ten hyperactive verbs. They look so happy, so spontaneous, so resilient.

No, verbs don't stay sad for long and they're never inactive. I will always see that moment. There's so much going on in the world – so much so right and so much so wrong. Regardless, I choose to see ten kids simply unclasping, breaking out of a huddle.

As for now, though my eyes are searching for that photographer.

I want a copy of that picture.

Writer's note: *I love happy endings and this story has one. Bryn not only went on to break 20 more than once in her high school career, but she's also now running club at UNC and is dangerously close to breaking 19 – at last check 19:06 was her new PR. Just thought you should know…*

LEMONADE FROM LEMONS

The year 2020 erased almost every normal in every category – the running world was no exception. In fact, it'd be quicker to talk about what WAS the same as opposed to what was different.

The "refresh" button on cell phones still got the living hell beat of them while parents, kids, and spectators waited for the results on Georgia Milesplit at the finish line. Separation Slope remained something to be reverently scared of. And, if you weren't scared enough, the media would be there at every turn to make sure you were fearing something…anything.

That season will forever etch in my mind as "The Art of Avoiding Getting Contact Traced," and we coached with a fear of, not being under or overtrained, but also over-exposed to someone with COVID. Still, this led to positive and simple solutions: Stay six feet away. Talk very fast. Then move on!

When, by the grace of God and every angel up there, the season did end, it was our banquet creativity, put together by our team moms, that will always stand out. Before going forward, I must say that team moms are the best inventions since sliced bread and the remote control. They take care of this, that, and this, while you all are free to coach.

But let's move on.

Indoors and buffet lines were out of the question as far as banquets – it was a germ thing - but that didn't stop our team from bringing lawn chairs and getting it done at the end of a cul de sac.

Think drive-in movie, without the risk of getting caught

sneaking kids in in your trunk. Picture a big screen, with wires running out of somebody's house and twisting and turning into one big box. Picture sitting back, munching on a burrito out of a sack, laughing at Jayaraj, reliving the season without having to worry about microphones working, or hiding presents under the podium.

The "movie" lasted an hour-and-a-half if anyone cared to time it, and I never even bothered to leave on purpose to go to the restroom. Imagine that as well, if you can.

In closing, yes it was a year of masks and guns and fewer coolers, but there were also spread out starting lines, resiliency, and the love for succeeding despite Las Vegas odds that said we couldn't. There was trying to pry apart kids who latch onto each other like ticks, saying goodbye to the handshake, and feeling guilty when hugging one of your conquering kids.

But, you know, there was a new appreciation - not just for the results - but for these kids getting past a hurdle thrown at them by the Heavens, surviving despite their norms wiped away by God's powerful eraser, as everything had to be written in pencil, not pen.

And there were still races and hills and turns and pain, shin splints and fartlek's and hill workouts, and PRs. There were pain and suffering, but there was survival of the fittest because we are the fittest.

And last, but not least, there was a season - a season that wasn't supposed to happen, yet it did. Starting guns that were refired. Cones set up each weekend and some during the week. And while life closed down for many, and the media scared all the rest, the runners of the world did what the runners of the world always do.

Endure.

THIS IS FUN...

I'm standing in the infield at a track meet, and I'm surrounded by adrenaline and chatter and heat sheets. There are kids warming up, others cooling down, coaches are urging and prodding and timing.

At about this moment, a coach from another school approached, and he had a reminiscent tone about him even though all this was happening before us if that makes any sense. Anyway, he said, "This is fun."

Another co-coach has a term for this, it's called a pure moment, a time when you don't want to be anywhere else other than where you are. With our traveling minds, it doesn't happen enough. Still...when it does...

Out of habit, my yellow pad and I move to the starting line, because there's nothing more energetic and expectant and hopeful than those young faces. Everything is in those expressions - from positivity, to let's get this over with, to some who are seemingly passing kidney stones.

And as runners know, there's nothing longer than that eternal second before that gun goes off - that silence even though there are hundreds of people there, that silence that is perhaps the loudest sound on earth.

On this day, at this track meet, I can't help but smile some more when I see such...normalcy going on again. Milesplit photographer Dan McCauley is taking massive pictures, Coach Jayaraj is recording splits and times and places and is happier than a 10-year-old on Christmas Eve. Kids are lacing them up, messing up formerly neat spike kits, putting in their earbuds to get themselves psyched.

I stand among this for eight hours without boredom, as my skin goes from frostbite to sunburn back to frostbite with the erratic Georgia weather. Still, there is this energy again that we so lost when we were all locked up, our mood dependent on news reports. There's this energy missing in Zoom school, though we're fortunate to have it in our technology-filled world. There's been this energy missing not being at a Saturday track meet.

My phone's ringing as I get home - it's my co-coach and friend. He's excited because our sophomore just dropped a 4:18 in the 1,600, and another broke two in the 800. Another one was a beast on the third leg of the 4 X 400, another has an injury that needs to be tended to.

As I open my trunk before going inside, there's a med kit there, a used spike kit, a yellow pad filled with numbers. The fact that most of the numbers are good is gravy as far as I'm concerned because this is a pad that collected dust for almost a year, the ink pen was filled and ready but there was no use for it.

Still, in closing, before I get inside, and before I condense eight hours at a track meet down to mere sentences, I can't get one sentence out of my head before I drifted off into dreamland. It was only one thought, and it was only three words.

This is fun...

MUST BE TRACK SEASON

A look at the Atlanta 10-day forecast calls for 70 degrees, warm and sunny one day, while dropping to 28, windy, and cold the next. Flash flood warnings are in effect Tuesday, followed by snow followed by balmy temperatures.

Only one thought pops into my head as I read this: Hmm, must be track season...

I stand now at practice, looking at these small, unathletic looking bodies - all angled and elbowed and slight. It makes me smile - at this sport and who and what it attracts. I try and picture if one were made to go out for football - picture him hitting the sled and falling backwards. Blocking the tackling dummy only to be tackled. Putting on the football letter jacket that's eight sizes too large.

After all, jackets our size have to be tailor made. I myself, just ordered a ring at girl size - the man-size version would be the "murder weapon special," covering all of my finger and most of my hand.

The kids chatter among themselves on this windy day - a day I need to put rocks in a couple of pockets to keep them from flying off into the pole vault pit. I do nothing to stop this talking, this flirting, syllables flying at 700 words per minute with gusts up to 1000.

Let them chatter; it's why I love this sport so much. This running thing - what we do and coach - is their own well-deserved ticket into athleticism, respect, letters, banquets, adulation and the like. Runners earn this in their own way, with suffering yet simplicity.

Most do it by running into each other, hitting a ball harder, exerting still more pressure. These kids do it inwardly, reaching still further and further inside. Inside - always inside. And in the end, though we've out-muscled and out-machoed absolutely no one, our trophy shines just as bright; the top rung of our podium still extends equally as high.

Running shoes. Shorts. A T-shirt. That's all that's required. On training days, boundaries aren't even needed. We have two rules: No one runs alone. And QUIT running in the neighbor's yards!

They will break both those rules, and often. Still, I smile. There's a weirdness to the track & field world that can't be duplicated. You either get it or you don't. Most people hear a gun fire and run for cover. Track coaches start their watches while goosebumps fill their arms.

In moving on, it's Valentine's Day as I write this. Still, the ones before me aren't handing out candy hearts or ordering bouquets from the nearest florist. Instead, they're laughing about the good deals they get if they wait until the 15th and get the chocolates for discount.

And the major questions of the day aren't dates and love and romance and roses. "Who's got the spike kit?" "How are we going to put the poles in that little van?" "Are we going to have enough to do the 4 X 400?"

For the record, it's cold and windy, soon to be erased by sunny, followed by flash floods. Yet for me, it's collecting bus keys, finding yellow legal pads to record times, eagerly await that beautiful sound of guns firing across Marietta and Roswell and Alpharetta and Rome. Watching pencil-thin kids' faces light up when they stare at their watches. Or limp off in tears.

Yes, it is track season.

And that, in itself, is a good thing...

BONGOS, SUPERSTITIONS, AND VIDEOTAPES

It seems one of our 3,200-meter runners – on race day – walks into the Riley Building at our school, goes to room 203, and turns on the Smart Board. He has a special song; puts it on the 3-minute mark and then plays the bongos.

I don't mean just plays the bongos, I mean he pounds the hell out of them until he's good and worked up. With that done, he then turns off the machine, walks out the door, and declares himself race ready.

It's the beauty of sports, the way kids go about things, the rituals they perform, the superstitions they create. It always angers me – this academics vs. athletics thing – because I can assure you kids learn from both, and why people have to take priority will always be beyond me.

Note to humans: Let kids learn in creative ways. It works!

The only issue, in my humble opinion, is that it's too much too soon, particularly when I see a coach videotaping a 10-year old regarding her form or her sport. You want to video tape a 10-year-old? Catch them playing hopscotch or peering over a Monopoly board on an odd Saturday night with her spend-the-night friends.

And may specializing among kids that age be cast into the hells that it came from.

But let's talk videotaping, while returning to my "bongo kid." He took his nervous energy to the track, ran a 9:52 in qualifying for Sectionals, slated for next week. But still, that's not the video! It seems his teammate –

who finished 10 seconds ahead of him – waited for him at the finish line, carried him off the track.

I witnessed this – Rocky and Apollo Creed, arm in arm, staggering off that track on a warm Atlanta night. The smiles, the teeth, the emotion, the EDUCATION. It wasn't a test they turned in and will soon forget, it was miles and trials and smiles – and tears – while working together.

But wait! Don't put the camera down – I've got another one. It seems we have this two-sport spring athlete, which in itself is the joy of high school sports. She's allowed to aid the soccer team to an Elite 8 finish on Wednesday, then be fully clad in track shoes and running attire the following day.

She was an alternate in the 4 X 800-relay on this day, but she showed up anyway. As things happened, one of the members had to pull out, and I had the job of telling the soccer/track girl she was going to get to run the 800.

I thought she was going to cry with joy. She jumped up and down – not kidding – and was SO happy she was GETTING TO RUN. Now this is not a girl who will be training for the Olympics down the road in track, there will be no coach correcting her form save her high school ones.

Still, the joy, the happiness, the thrill of running!

This is your education people – and it is education in every sense of the word. There are two of your video moments.

And these two events aren't tapes I'll put in a drawer and forget due to tomorrow's agenda. These are videos I will never forget, and quite simply, can never be erased.

FOR THE LOVE OF THE RUN

This is a speech I convinced myself to give back in the summer of 2019 – regarding Smoky Mountain Running Camp in Asheville. Hopefully – even if you've never attended – you'll get something out of it.

My first year here back in 2004 was my first introduction to what you all did this morning: Buzzard Bait. A counselor drew a line in the sand with his foot, pointed up, and told us not to worry. After all, there was only one hill. He laughed at his joke. We did not. Neither did you.

I, like you, felt I ran so high that when I prayed to God, I actually looked down instead of up, faced one switch back after another, my Tourette's Syndrome kicked in so bad I offended everyone and anyone near me. I ran by a guy praising Jesus, I cussed so bad he thought I was the devil. Still, I, like you, like him, made it to the top.

And to this day it's a badge of honor, something I flex like a muscle, wear like an Olympic medal. I stand here before you a man who has flunked history, been thrown out of my house by my ex-wife, went to my high school homecoming with one date and came home with another, and even fell through the roof of my very own school – while it was in session.

But I have run Buzzard Bait. I have done Smoky Mountain Running Camp. On purpose. Year after year. And I to this day see those people at races across Georgia and beyond, see the SMRC T-shirts when running at the river, recognize your faces at starting and finish lines, and I will smile. Yes, that's me, the old man you don't know who always waves and points at you as I waddle by.

Don't worry. I'm harmless. I just appreciate a good bond when I have one. And I appreciate the love of the run.

It's funny how when speakers are introduced, they say nice things about the person. As for me, I also stand before you the coach who presided over the worst pacing contest group in the 40-plus year history of SMRC. My co-coach blamed it on me. Being an honorable soul if nothing else, I blame it on that bear we saw while running the day before at the Warren Wilson ball fields.

We turned a corner and there he was – not that big but still, a bear, nonetheless. In retreating, it was the fastest run in camp history by a group 19. Still I, out of respect for Coach Benson and Coach Drosky and their rules, made sure they sprinted back to the bus going 2-by-2. Nobody gets ahead of the leader; nobody lags behind the sweeper. They did all that, for the record, though I can assure you no one was behind the sweeper.

It was just me and the bear; fortunately it was the first and only race I've ever won in my life.

Unfortunately, the adrenaline continued the next day in the pacing contest when our youth ran the mile at about 1:40 too fast, leaving my illustrious group so far off the podium I was muted the next three years while helping out with the pacing. Just keep the time I was told. Just stand way over there and keep the time. Just yell numbers but no instruction.

But I digress.

This passion started for me way before cell phones, computers, text messaging; even before the Goldberg's and the Big Bang Theory, but not before Jerry Crockett was born. My dad was a miler at the University of New Hampshire; took me aside one day, told me not to go out too fast when running my first 3,200-meter race, then known simply as the 2-mile.

Sporting new blue basketball shoes, heavy shorts and some newly acquired zits, off I went – way too fast – as you all probably did on your first race. Still, something happened during those eight laps – besides boredom – and finishing far from first. I was on to something – something simple. No equipment required, just run. No grips, not too many fundamentals, just left foot, right foot, repeat.

One day, while disguised as a married man in Florida, somebody mentioned a running camp in Asheville. Asheville, the Berkeley of the South, where locals, hippies, and tourists all gather and somehow it all works. Still, locals, hippies, and tourists, and a running camp? Really?

It was here I saw a Nike rep propose to his wife, watched Jerry Crockett turn younger every year, almost got killed by lightning along with Andy Carr, saw someone actually get lost on Buzzard Bait even though there's only one road, and enjoyed some of the finest, 5-star, drool-infested naps in SMRC history. And the smoothies aren't bad either, coming in second only to the late-night conversations in the hospitality room, conversations I've sworn in blood I'll never write or tell in public.

My wife at the time, not a runner, didn't understand when I returned home. Being over 40 back then, I was tired of explaining to non-runners what it is we do, who it is we are. I just looked at her and said, "Look, it's like this. SMRC is a roller coaster ride, except the place where you get off is a very different place from where you got on."

Yeah, that.

Every year here is like that. Every camp since 2004. I

drive away different, touched, branded and bonded. Still, the beauty is, there's no superiority in this sport in my humble opinion. My sweat is no better or worse than yours. We just keep moving forward – first-and-10, new set of downs, move the chains. In my tennis days, you could win or lose 6-0, 6-0 and feel a sense of superiority over or below your opponent. In this sport, whether you run a 15 minute or 30-minute 5K, you still push yourself, sweat, suffer.

When you cross the finish line you've just bonded with 100-plus people, or however many were in the race. You did it!

Sometimes back home I get accused for not going to church enough. Church? I feel I find God when I run at the Lower Arboretum, pass the wood chip trail, run by the trestle, cross the bridge, take a left onto the trail. One year there was a snake in the way; I was on such a natural high I just went right passed him, slithered on forwards while he slithered sideways. Sometimes I find God in the bamboo at the ball field trail. And he laughs at me when I get my group lost at the church. Hmm, maybe that's my punishment.

Running Camp. Buzzard Bait. Mills Dorms. Do I have the extra dessert at dining hall? Talking after light's out. Getting dressed up for the pacing contest. Hoping you get top-5; or at least not last. Break-outs. Thunder and lightning storms. Coach O's speeches, always something about fluids. And cups. And don't forget the coolers.

There are books to be written about camp – both before lights out and after. I'll just smile, appreciate and write neither one. Probably because I'm guilty in at least half the stories, but mainly because I always want to be invited back. It started 15 years ago as a flippant idea, something to do to get away from my wife before she threw me out. Now it's become a part of my very soul.

You either get it or you don't. And trust me, don't try to convince people who don't. They look at you funny, tilt their head, ask why you do it, make you feel as if you have some disease. They actually back off you a bit where they won't catch it. Doctors have told me to stop, I'm pushing 60. My back flips me off constantly when I'm trying to do the simple chore of putting on my socks.

Still, I'm standing in a place that literally helped save my life. I celebrated my marriage here, and later my divorce. Learned I didn't have prostate cancer while here. Celebrated with my roommate when he found out his wife was pregnant. I also kept him from jumping out the 7th story window, but perhaps that's another story.

One run at a time. One kid at a time. One story at a time. Little by little, my own bout with a clinical depression began to lift while here back in 2008 – as a year before I had to stay home it was so bad. Morgan Freeman said it in the movie Shawshank Redemption, "get busy living or get busy dying."

Living, always living – and the love of the run, particularly the camp runs. Like this one: On one SMRC Monday morning, a stray dog – unassigned by Coach Scott or Tillery to us – joined Group 12. The question came up, a question that can only arise among runners: Multiplying the dogs age by 7 since that's how they age, if we were racing is he in our age group? Do we risk a kick to beat him on a Monday, with three more runs, pacing contest, and Buzzard Bait still to go? Another question: Was it male or female? Do we stop the group and turn the dog over? Also, does the dog bite?

And other run, after lecturing my kids on leaving a

gap between them and being careful, I proceeded to get them lost at the Upper Arboretum, while getting bit by a wasp, while tripping in front of my entire group and falling flat on my face. I think that's when it hit me: "This is fun. It's great to be back in the world again. I'm ready for almost anything – except maybe Buzzard Bait."

The love of the run. Coaching great kids. Soaking up your energy and adrenaline. Watching you all try to flirt. Getting lost on Mule Trail. Trying in vain to read one of Coach O's maps to keep from getting lost at the church. Listening to the meeting on bee stings, yet grateful I've never had to pull out an epi-pen or pee on any one of you people to this very day.

Maybe I'll close this way, because this to me defines what we do and who we are. Will leave you with a seemingly random moment in time, if there is such a thing.

Anyway, as a coach, one of my senior runners at Holy Innocents' crossed the finish line at the JV race at Wesleyan a few years ago. She didn't inherit the correct genes for the sport, her times wouldn't turn any heads.

Still, on that day my heart sank while at the same time lifted at what I saw in this very sport. You see, when she crossed that finish line she broke into tears. It was her last race. Her being a part of a team, wearing the uniform, putting on a bib number, waking up early on a cross country Saturday morning, and crossing the finish lines were all over.

She had joined the team out of peer pressure, something to do, maybe as a pause from studying or to keep her from watching too much TV.

Not caring about political correctness or appearances, I walked over and I hugged her – right there at the finish line. After all, she got it. Probably still does. What we do climbed right past her personal fitness and became a part of her. Yes, I get perceptions, PR stuff, appearances, heck I right the articles myself.

Still, I'm glad I met her at the finish line that day. After all, sometimes – if not all the time – you have to put your role as a human being ahead of your role in your job. And whenever you're around people who get it, you have to love that, never forget that, realize it's a connector factor that will never fade.

Getting to more present day, my back shot me the proverbial bird back in January. Went for a run and was paralyzed trying to get out of my car. Doctors told me to quit running – oh those silly humans – but I instead went through X-rays, sat in enclosed tubes for 20 minutes straight even though I'm claustrophobic times 12, took Epidural injections, went to rehab and still do, and now ride the bus to the top of Buzzard Bait.

No reason for you to know who I am, I'm a passing face who gave you water, told you to put your bagel wrapper in the trash, gave you knucks for a job well done. Still, as I drive home, I will do so in appreciation for what you've done, who you are, and the sport you're in. Will gather my own team a short week from now in preparing for another season.

As you get older, you live your life through the young, it's your world. Still, on odd days when the schedule isn't tight and my back is a little loose, while the young ones are off running and flirting and gabbing before getting back to the vans, my shoes and shorts will be in the trunk.

Using the time more than well, flipping my own proverbial bird at old age, remembering my love for SMRC and this sport we do, I will reach into my trunk.

And with my bonds and memories of bee stings, bears, a dogs age group, Seinfeld episodes in Mills commons, standing on and below the pacing group podium and beyond, I will put on my shoes.

I will lace them up.

And with a smile on my face, I will run…

PART III: THE FINISH LINE

MY GREATEST VICTORY!

An Anatomy of an Illness

You're lying on the couch – for the second hour, or fifth, or the eighth – you're not sure. What's it matter; lifelessness has no agenda. You think you hear music from your upstairs neighbor; you roll over, tune it out.

Why shouldn't you; your station has been on mute for quite a while now.

Eventually – maybe it's couch sores, maybe it's boredom and inertia times twelve but…for whatever reason… you do the hardest thing ever, whether it's running, writing, or living…

You get up. Take the first step.

Life is out there, but it's passing you by. You're on autopilot once at school; you walk down the hall, head down. You think there is chattering going on but you're not sure – it's muffled – as if you're underwater.

As the saying goes, you chop wood, carry water, stand in lines, fill out forms. Exist.

One day, as you're headed off to class you hear people singing, some on-key and some off, but still…singing. You stop at the doorway of Room 406 in amusement. There is a history teacher, a Spanish teacher, a golfer, cheerleader and a nerd. One is playing the piano, another the guitar, some simply stare at the Smartboard and sing.

It's bad, but it's good all the same. You don't join in, you can't. Still, if nothing else, a note pad is grabbed in your mind, pencil moves to paper. After all – if nothing else – you couldn't help noticing how cute that scene was, how…cohesive.

Still, you move away from the sounds.

You're at carpool now and you're freezing your butt off, the 25 mile per hour winds not giving one damn about the four layers you have on. Instead, the rain teams with the wind and they rip a steady hole in the side of your face. You miss your dog, or your lost loved one, or your best friend, or your old job. Whatever is ailing you.

The hole is still there and maybe forever will be. You can't hear the music. But then, a car stops, holding up the line. A window rolls down, a hand reaches out. It's a cup of coffee. A parent brought it for you, how…incredibly thoughtfully nice.

You walk up, take it, not feeling you deserve it. Still, wow. You watch while the car drives down the line – that lady with her kid and the dog in the backseat. As the car exits, the lady lowers her window in spite of the crappy weather, gives you a smile, tells you to have a nice day.

Your shift ends and you walk back inside. There's a tad faster gait to your step, almost as if you can hear the music. The music? Room 406 is two buildings away, yet it's there, maybe it was there all along. You're not sure – the notes are coming in and out – perhaps an AM radio on static if you will.

Regardless, you notice girls braiding each other's hair, boys throwing shit at each other, some talking trash about their Fantasy Football team. Teachers try to shoo them all to class, bells are ringing, and you can't help but notice there just may be a bit of order to this chaos.

You stop, watch, take it in. Somewhere in the back of your mind, clamoring for attention, you can sense a bit of rhythm, dots connecting.

One day, you're trying to recall just how you took that first step – and perhaps why – but you're still up, about. And on that day, it happens. There are two talking, right there, by the second set of lockers. They look…energetic, happy…embraceful though that's not even a word.

Still, you do something you haven't done in 16 months. You walk over and you join them. You can't help but notice as you approach, one of them moves, just a tad, a couple of inches – off to the side.

He let you in. He let you in. You wonder how a two to six inch gesture can be so huge, matter so much. After all, people move everywhere, all the time. Still, you're…in. You contribute nothing to the conversation, still, you are present. There.

Eventually this one goes this way, that one that, and there's a humming inside your head as you remember that you, too, have some place to be. Hopefully God is sitting down for this, but a smile touches your face, cracks a bit – like the first step of a jog when you forgot to stretch.

Still, wow, a smile…A conversation. Inclusion.

Something happens at practice later that week. You can't help but notice…the energy. The way they flirt during stretch line, giggle while doing a burpee, gossip while the coach isn't looking. Agendas are everywhere, little lives, voices, chatter, worlds colliding with worlds.

You say nothing, even though as coach you're supposed to. Instead you simply walk down the line, listen, soak it up. Energy, it's really out there. That's your thought as an old favorite song plays inside your head, one you heard in college, the one where you fantasized about being on stage in front of thousands.

You try to shrug it off as a fantasy, then you realize that even fantasies can, too, lend a hand. You smile, you almost laugh, as you walk back to the front of the line and address your team.

One day you realize that maybe your situation is like running the mile. Lap one – you think you can't do it, scared to move. Lap 2 – like it or not, you just get with the program. Chop wood. Carry water. Lap 3…Can you do this? Maybe you really are tuning in.

And now one day you're at a finish line, there's so much adrenaline you can't even hold your note pad. Your beautiful kids are out there – somewhere – climbing hills, tromping through ice and mud, hurting, suffering.

You've felt their pain in a different way, a part of it will always invite itself in at times. Still, you smile at the fact that the shit storms are less intense now, less frequent. You push the thoughts away – passing clouds if you will – and simply appreciate while those wonderful souls come hauling butt down that hill.

You watch them hold on to each other. Help each other up. Giggle and cry all together. They did so well you pump your fist into the air, look up at God.

This time, though, you don't laugh, but instead you cry. And pretty embarrassingly hard. So much so you have to bend over and grab both your knees.

Still, you almost walk on air back to those kids, that energy, this life. You realize sometimes you make no footprints when you move – you're being carried. You appreciate that, words can't say how much you really appreciate that.

As you walk with your kids back to your tent, the sounds of Room 406 fill your head. It's not on-key but it doesn't have to be – that's the way it is when little angels play their songs – each singing their own part. It's chaotic, then again, it's not. It's really not.

Anyway, there's a huddle going on when you reach the people at your tent, as if Room 406 invited every other room to the dance – all seem to be here at this finish line celebration.

You hesitate at first, taking it all in. Then, with a smile on your face and tears in your eyes, you walk in rhythm into the middle of it all…

PART IV: A VICTORY LAP

A VALENTINE'S TALE – A STORY OF LOVE AND OF LIKE

Writer's Warning: *This story has nothing to do with running. Like the title says, it's a story of love and of like, the history of meeting my girlfriend, combined with meeting my very own self. It's also a story of gratitude, in that sometimes you do get second chances. And finally, I love happy endings and so far, this one is very happy. Personally, I've never cared for drama – the man and the woman are always supposed to end up walking hand in hand on the beach while the sun sets and the credits roll. There. Simple. The End.*

I met her at a party in 1984. Normally tongue-tied when seeing someone attractive, this time – for whatever reason – I wasn't. Abruptly ending my conversation, I walked over and put my arm around her.

For the rest of the night, I didn't let her go. For some reason, she didn't seem to mind.

We dated some but you must get the picture. I was 24 going on 7 – much too "young" to be in an adult relationship. Naturally, I screwed it up time and again and eventually she moved on. Who could blame her? As for me, my thought process was something like this: How can she be that good a woman if she likes me?

Yes, I was that bad. And when the moon was tilted right, I was worse.

Fast forward to last decade, living in Florida. My wife had just told me she didn't like me anymore. That was fine, I didn't like me either, never had. In what hopefully was my lowest point on planet earth, I had a breakdown when I heard "Ain't No Sunshine When She's Gone" blaring out of those speakers in that Jupiter, Florida townhome. My dog was concerned. So was I. It bothered me that no one else was.

In a moment I'm least proud, I looked up at that Florida sky and I cussed at the heavens. "This (bleep) stops right here. Right NOW!" It was rock bottom; I had no choice but to get up again.

God took me seriously. It was time I did, too. And so began my fixation. After all, every relationship starts with yourself, right? How can you love anything when you're filled with self-filth? It was time to get comfortable, not in my own shoes, but in my own head.

So for the first time in my life, I studied. Norman Vincent Peale. Alan Cohen. Louise Hay. Esther Hicks. Joel Osteen. Pam Grout. Deepak Chopra. I got lost 10 times but I met Wayne Dyer - twice. I didn't give a damn about anything; I was going to fix myself. Period.

Tapes. Seminars. Subliminal Messages. Books. Novels be damned.

Moving on, I'm back in Atlanta. Job is good. Kids are great. Condo so far has withstood every storm. I'm living large with my pet roaches. I'm drinking my beer – self-hatred or otherwise, I do love my beer – and something catches my eye on Facebook.

It was something my oldest brother, Chip, wrote, but it was what was under it that sobered me. "Sheryl Alford Murphy liked this." Sheryl Alford Murphy? That was…her…

Do I hit "send friend request?" Should I? She loves me, she loves me not. Was I a man or my pet roach? I wasn't exactly the man of the year in the 80s, had she forgotten? Was she forgiving?

I hit "send," closed my computer, put down my beer, went to sleep.

She accepted, we met for a drink at Meehan's. Life hadn't aged her a day. Three kids and she's still picture perfect, fit, young, vibrant and pretty. Still laughs so easily. This fits my ego; I often try to be funny.

Yes, I almost reverted, almost screwed it up all over again. This time I caught myself, remembered all the words I've read, all the studying I've done, no degree needed. No, I still can't follow Louise Hay's advice; I can't look myself in the mirror and say, "I love you."

The best I can come up with is "You're going to go out looking like THAT!"

Still, I'm going to see her for Valentine's Day later and I can't wait. Can't wait to hear that staccato laugh of hers, the way she leans her head forward when she does it. The simple things – if you've read anything I've ever written, you know I love simple things.

Oh, and before I close, back to the question: How can she be a good woman if she likes me?

Answer: Regardless of what she thinks of me, she's the best. It is that simple.

And as for me, I think I've almost graduated from my studies – I've written my one sentence thesis and I'm going to share it right here in front of the former God I cussed at, the God I love, and everyone on Facebook:

I love her, I like you all, and I'm really not so bad myself…

Happy Valentine's Day…every day…

THE COOL DOWN

Looking back, the cosmic joke is that it's not really that complicated. Find your passion. Focus there. Follow your good thoughts, go where they lead. Take only **positively** focused action – otherwise you're not only spinning your wheels, but you're probably going backwards.

The run is over, for now. I hope reading this finds you lacing up your shoes, changing out your spikes, or writing down your race goal. Don't just think it, mind you – write it down! Writing it down makes it real, whereas you can always lie to yourself if you just spin it through your head.

Don't give yourself that option. Make. It. Real.

I write, run, and coach from what I call a circle. Track season leads to summer cross country running which leads to cross country season which leads to winter track training which leads to track season again. The trick is to enjoy the circle, revel in it, let it move you for better and for worse. Or perhaps I should say for faster and for slower.

Years ago, as I led these tales off with, I traded my passions – took off my Stan Smith tennis shoes, stowed away my Prince tennis racket, and went – a babe in the woods – to a running camp in North Carolina. I can assure you; I was by far the dumbest kid in every room I entered. Still, I loved it.

I always know when something moves me to put pen to paper that I'm on to something – something that needs more information, needs investigating. Later, and in what was either the process of elimination or because I had a marathon under my belt – I was named cross country coach at my school.

More than nervous, I went to Barnes & Noble, checked out books, talked to people, sweated bullets, fidgeted in my sleep, saw myself crashing and burning in front of coaches and runners who all knew more than me.

Then I read this: It seems a man went to his guru for this very reason – he'd taken a job he wasn't sure he could handle. Would they respect him? Would people see right through him? Who was he to take the job anyway?

The guru smiled and said, "You don't need to worry about any of that. Unless you're working for NASA or somewhere like that, you can learn what you need to know on the fly. All you have to do is love the people you're working with, love the people you're around, and then everything will take care of itself."

I laughed at that when I first read it – now I know it to be true. And for me, though I'll never be close to the Nick Saban of running, I am around great people day in and day out, and not just within my own school system. Runners are cerebral people; they can go within at the sound of a starting gun and out again when crossing the tape.

But, like kids, they are real. My job, at the point of taking the position, was to make myself someone that could be seen inside and out and remain someone I could present to the world without shame, with no remorse.

Once the race is on, after all, your resume doesn't really matter anymore. You sweat as I do. You hurt as I do. You suffer as I do. Our sweat is wet and our blood is red. It's a level playing surface if you will, regardless of how hilly.

So, I close this book and these little tales as someone who has crossed this particular finish line. I close with so much to learn, and for everything I learn it lets me know how much I actually have to go.

Still, that's running. There really is no finish line. Yet, once upon a time there was this scared coach who took a position that he was underqualified for. He met his assistants and then his kids and then other coaches. He ran in packs with kids and adults. He often ran alone because he needed to. He went to camps and seminars, read up on it.

And to this very day, he walks away with a smile on his face, passion in his heart, and respect in his brain for this world, this running thing, this sport. This man is looking down now, looking at his watch, turning it off because this race is over.

At this stage of the game, however, he smiles no matter what his time reads, so instead of his mood depending on the numbers on his watch, these days he simply puts his running shoes where they can be found the next day, and the next.

After all, and as the movie once said, 'Tomorrow is another day.'

Thanks for listening…

–Dunn Neugebauer

Spring 2021

ACKNOWLEDGEMENTS

My first thank you goes to the embracing community I have found that is the running world. You either get it or you don't, and though I'm never here to crack on the ones who don't, instead I'm thankful I'm around the ones who do.

I'm recalling a conversation a week before I was entered in the Chicago Marathon, trying to qualify for Boston. "You mean, you have paid for your air flight, hotel room, race fee, and you're flying up to Chicago just to run 26.2 miles?!"

"Yes, and I can't wait to do it," was my reply.

"But why?"

Here's the thing: I couldn't answer that because the reasons vary. Once something is in your blood, explanations are unnecessary, not required. You just do what you do because it's a place where you can both shift into high physical and mental gear in competition or you can drift off into nowhere land in your mind, solve problems in your head, write essays.

So thanks to you all.

And thanks to my co-coach and friend, Stephen Jayaraj, who for three years has been saying, "You need to put all these essays into a book!" Well Stephen, as you might have surmised by now, sometimes it takes a while for things to penetrate that iron block that sits on top of my neck, and it's tough to get past the pizzas, TV dinners, and agendas that cram themselves into my skull and down my throat.

Still, I did it, and like running, I set no records and didn't PR, but I had a good time, if not a good, recorded time if you know what I mean.

And finally, thanks for reading. Writing can be a lonely world; you reach for a pen at 2:30 in the morning out of inspiration, fire down thoughts that you can't wait to bring to life, and often, most often, you do it simply and only for the love of doing it, the passion for the craft.

Running and life are the same to me in that way and so many others. Still, to strip me of my running shoes and my pen would be imprisonment, solitary confinement even if I were around the masses.

Enough from me, I've taken up enough of your time. Though the finish line isn't reached and I'm thankful it never will be, this particular race is over. And, like all the rest of them, no sooner have I recorded my times, splits, races, and paces, there's another one brewing inside my head.

After all, there will always be tracks out there, timers, officials, people in the chute, or perhaps just the beauty of a Sunday morning trail zigging and zagging me into no place in particular.

Keep it coming. Gives me goosebumps just thinking about it…

Arigato!

YOU ARE CORDIALLY INVITED... TO WRITE A REVIEW

If you've made it to this finish line, I would love it if you'd take the 22 seconds or so to write a review. I get it, many are intimidated by the idea of putting their own thoughts down on paper. After all, once they do it, it's OUT THERE.

Still, it can be as simple as one or two sentences. Here's an example from a friend who read this: "I can tell just by looking over this book that the school Dunn works for keeps forgetting to run him through the metal detector. Regardless, he really does mean well and he tries hard, so I'm going to give him five stars just for the effort."

See? That wasn't so hard. And I can tell you from my heart that I completely appreciated my friend's accurate criticism and his comment.

Also, I'm a self-publishing man who works at a school. Word of mouth and reviews are the way to go as far as getting us "little guys" out there. Facebook, Instagram, and Twitter, you see, can only do so much.

So thanks in advance.

And in closing, if you feel so inclined, don't hesitate to send me an email at: dunn.neugebauer@hies.org. Please keep it Rated G as this is a school system mail and Big Brother may or may not be watching.

ABOUT THE AUTHOR

Dunn Neugebauer came up as a tennis player, but eventually took up the joys of running without having to worry about holding a racket or keeping score. A columnist for Georgia Milesplit and author of three other books, he currently coaches cross country and track at a high school in Atlanta, where the teams remain state contenders year after year, including a state cross country title in 2019. When not writing or running, Dunn enjoys the art of simply observing life as he knows it, as opposed to staring at his cell phone for hours on end. He lives in Sandy Springs and is often seen running at dump truck pace on the nearby Chattahoochee River trails.